MAXnotes®

Daniel Defoe's

Moll Flanders

Text by
Susan E. Gallagher
(M.A., New School for Social Research)

Dr. M. Fogiel
Chief Editor

Illustrations by
Kenneth Lopez

Research & Education Association

MAXnotes® for
MOLL FLANDERS

Copyright © 1996 by Research & Education Association. All rights reserved. No part of this book may be reproduced in any form without permission of the publisher.

Printed in the United States of America

Library of Congress Catalog Card Number 96-67426

International Standard Book Number 0-87891-031-X

MAXnotes® is a registered trademark of
Research & Education Association, Piscataway, New Jersey 08854

What **MAXnotes®** Will Do for You

This book is intended to help you absorb the essential contents and features of Daniel Defoe's *Moll Flanders* and to help you gain a thorough understanding of the work. The book has been designed to do this more quickly and effectively than any other study guide.

For best results, this **MAXnotes** book should be used as a companion to the actual work, not instead of it. The interaction between the two will greatly benefit you.

To help you in your studies, this book presents the most up-to-date interpretations of every section of the actual work, followed by questions and fully explained answers that will enable you to analyze the material critically. The questions also will help you to test your understanding of the work and will prepare you for discussions and exams.

Meaningful illustrations are included to further enhance your understanding and enjoyment of the literary work. The illustrations are designed to place you into the mood and spirit of the work's settings.

The **MAXnotes** also include summaries, character lists, explanations of plot, and section-by-section analyses. A biography of the author and discussion of the work's historical context will help you put this literary piece into the proper perspective of what is taking place.

The use of this study guide will save you the hours of preparation time that would ordinarily be required to arrive at a complete grasp of this work of literature. You will be well prepared for classroom discussions, homework, and exams. The guidelines that are included for writing papers and reports on various topics will prepare you for any added work which may be assigned.

The **MAXnotes** will take your grades "to the max."

Dr. Max Fogiel
Program Director

Contents

Section One: *Introduction* 1
   The Life and Work of Daniel Defoe 1
   Historical Background 3
   Master List of Characters 6
   Summary of the Novel 7
   Estimated Reading Time 9

> **Each Part includes List of Characters, Summary, Analysis, Study Questions and Answers, and Suggested Essay Topics.**

Section Two: *Moll Becomes a "Gentlewoman"* 10
   Preface 10
   Part One: Moll's Early Life 11
   Part Two: "The Ordeal of Virtue" 15

Section Three: *Moll's Early Adventures in Marriage* 20
  Part Three: The Draper 20
  Part Four: An Unnatural Alliance 23

Section Four: *Moll's Later Adventures In and Out of Marriage* 30
  Part Five: A Sinful Affair 30
  Part Six: Jemy 34
  Part Seven: The Governess and the Banker 38

Section Five: *Adventures in Crime* 46
  Part Eight: Early Success 46
  Part Nine: Close Calls 50
  Part Ten: Captured 53

Section Six: *Repentance and Prosperity* 62
  Part Eleven: Newgate Prison 62
  Part Twelve: A Happy Reunion 67
  Part Thirteen: Off to America 69
  Part Fourteen: Rich at Last 72

Section Seven: *Sample Analytical Paper Topics* 80

Section Eight: *Bibliography* 84

SECTION ONE

Introduction

The Life and Work of Daniel Defoe

Born in London in 1660, Daniel Defoe became one of the most productive and versatile writers in British history. His works included, along with novels such as *Moll Flanders* and *Robinson Crusoe*, hundreds of political tracts and pamphlets, books on history, economics, and geography, as well as guides to family living and business success. For many years, Defoe single-handedly produced his own newspaper, the *Review*, which dealt with topics ranging from the social implications of crime to the scientific aspects of astrology.

Despite his remarkable energy, Defoe never escaped the economic insecurity that characterized his early life. Because his father, James Foe, a butcher and candlemaker, dissented from the teachings of the Church of England, the family was denied access to established business and political circles and faced constant economic distress. In an effort to procure a better life for their son, Defoe's parents sent him to study at Newington Green, a well-known school for religious dissenters, where they hoped he would prepare for a career as a Presbyterian minister. However, in 1679, after five years of study, Defoe left school to try his hand in the clothing trade.

Thanks in part to a large dowry (£3,700) he received upon marrying Mary Tuffley in 1684, Defoe became a relatively prosperous tradesman for nearly a decade. Around this time, he began to sign himself as de Foe or Defoe, an alteration that lent his family name a somewhat aristocratic air. Unfortunately, when war with

France broke out in 1692, Defoe's business suffered major losses. He was forced into bankruptcy and narrowly escaped imprisonment for debt. While slowly paying off his creditors, he managed to invest in a small tile factory. However, even though his writings on trade display great insight into the principles of modern commerce, he failed to achieve his own economic success.

While pursuing his business interests, Defoe served as a secret agent and propagandist for William of Orange, a Protestant who occupied the throne from 1688 until 1702. Defoe produced a steady stream of pamphlets in support of the King's policies. However, rather than establishing himself as an advocate for the Whigs, the more progressive party in eighteenth-century British politics, or aligning himself with the Tories, who tended toward more conservative views, Defoe alienated influential leaders on both sides. Soon after Queen Anne succeeded William, Defoe was charged with high crimes and misdemeanors for writing *The Shortest Way with the Dissenters*, a satire on religious intolerance. He spent three months in Newgate Prison where, with his usual resourcefulness, he seized the opportunity to explore the social and psychological characteristics of his fellow inmates.

Defoe's incarceration destroyed the last remnants of his small fortune. In order to save his family from complete destitution, he struck a deal with a powerful politician and agreed to write the *Review* in support of the policies of the Tory government. A few years later, when the Whigs came to power, Defoe quickly switched to their party line. From then on, it became clear that Defoe was willing to write for anyone who would pay him for his service. While generally known as a Tory, he secretly authored dozens of pro-Whig tracts and pamphlets, a practice which allowed him to sustain himself as a political journalist, but placed him in constant danger of exposure and arrest.

In late middle age, Defoe turned to novel writing. His first and most famous novel, *Robinson Crusoe*, was published in 1719 and, over the next three years, he produced two more great works of fiction, *Moll Flanders* and *A Journal of the Plague Year*. The familiarity of Defoe's characters, the clarity of his prose, and the riveting adventures described in his stories made his work both accessible and appealing to a new segment of the reading public,

Introduction

the expanding middle class. Though critics have often faulted him for his tendency to dwell on vulgar subjects, the way his narratives explore the psychological motivations of unified and believable characters has earned him a widely accepted reputation as the first authentic novelist.

Many of Defoe's works, both fiction and nonfiction, were popular in his time. His literary accomplishments did not, however, protect him from his creditors. During the final years of his life, Defoe attempted to evade the demands of debt collectors by hiding out in a boarding house in Ropemaker's Alley in London. He died there, harried until the end, in 1731.

Historical Background

During Defoe's lifetime, commercial development transformed the social, economic, and political structure of Great Britain. The founding of the Bank of England, the rise of the stock market, and the growth of huge trading companies between the 1690's and 1730's laid the financial groundwork for the subsequent evolution of the British empire. As Defoe observed in his *Tour Through the Whole Island of Great Britain*, at the beginning of the eighteenth century, crowds of eager investors poured into London hoping to strike it rich in Exchange Alley, the side street in which stockjobbers (later known as brokers) plied their trade. Reflecting on the feverish speculation in stocks and the craze for financial schemes that characterized this period, Defoe concluded that British society had entered what he termed the "Projecting Age."

This new commercial spirit pervades Defoe's work. In his economic pamphlets, such as *Giving Alms No Charity* (1704) and *The Complete English Tradesman* (1732), Defoe defended the pursuit of economic self-interest both as an individual right and as an exercise of personal responsibility. Against the aristocratic notion that property should be gained and maintained mainly through inheritance, he argued that access to riches ought to be determined by the ability of individuals to plan carefully, work diligently, and take full advantage of every opportunity to accumulate additional wealth. In light of these assertions, Defoe has often been singled out as one of the cardinal spokesmen for modern capitalism, that is, an economic system in which the fate of individuals is controlled by their capacity to respond to market forces, rather than dictated strictly by their social class.

While Defoe seemed to celebrate economic self-interest in many of his essays, his novels and other occasional writings explore the irrational aspects of the pursuit of private gain. In *Robinson Crusoe*, for example, the protagonist, a man shipwrecked alone on a desert island, keeps an account book in which he carefully balances the positive elements of his situation against the negative aspects of his fate. Despite his isolation from the rest of society, Crusoe behaves as if he were living under the financial pressures of life in London, and he constantly reduces his destiny to entirely economic terms. On the basis of this purely materialistic mode of thinking, the character of Robinson Crusoe has often been interpreted as a model of modern commercial consciousness.

Likewise, in *Moll Flanders* and a somewhat similar novel, *Roxanna*, the title characters constantly calculate financial gains and losses. Unlike Robinson Crusoe, however, these two characters are not merely materialistic. Instead, Moll Flanders and Roxanna both commit terrible crimes in their efforts to satisfy their avarice and ambition; moreover, both are so consumed by greed that neither comprehends the consequences of her depraved behavior. Thus, despite his frequently optimistic comments on commercial progress, Defoe seems to have shared at least some of the anti-commercial sentiments expressed by many of the moralists of his day. The portraits of moral corruption presented in *Moll Flanders* and *Roxanna* illustrate that, like many other writers in eighteenth century Britain, including Jonathan Swift, Alexander Pope, and Henry Fielding, Defoe worried that increasing economic competition would cause individuals to become so intent on getting and spending that they would no longer be able to distinguish between good and evil.

In keeping with the sense of moral confusion inspired by commercial development, the reading public in this period developed a near obsession with the exploits of ingenious criminals, especially those who managed to amass great wealth. Thus, like Henry Fielding, Defoe wrote an account of the career of Jonathan Wild, one of the richest and most colorful criminals of the age. Wild's cunning schemes and daring capers became objects of widespread fascination, not only because they were creative and audacious, but because they seemed to exemplify the slick intelligence required to achieve commercial success. The methods Wild used to con his victims were accordingly likened both to those of stockbrokers who lured in investors with talk of easy money and to those of politicians who lined their own pockets while pretending to serve the interests of their country.

That Defoe published his biography of Wild soon after he wrote *Moll Flanders* makes a great deal of sense. In both works, Defoe was attempting to exploit popular interest in criminal behavior and also to explore the increasingly slippery nature of property-ownership. The explosive growth of the stock market during the first few decades of the eighteenth century enabled entrepreneurs to found companies, build places of business, hire workers, and carry out projects merely by promising investors attractive returns. This new system of production, trade, and profit-making meant not only that fortunes could be made overnight, but that wealth could evaporate just as quickly if investor confidence faltered, a purely psychological and often wildly unpredictable event.

Given this degree of uncertainty, many eighteenth-century social observers concluded that the success or failure of individuals depended not so much on their moral integrity as on the way they presented themselves to society. Social status thus seemed to hinge not on what individuals actually did, but only on the way their actions were perceived. Throughout *Moll Flanders*, the heroine and the rest of the characters accordingly worry only about appearances; rather than questioning whether their actions are truly good or truly bad, they are troubled only about the way their actions are or might be received. Moreover, since just about all of the characters in the novel adopt this shallow mentality, Defoe's message seems to be that indifference toward morality is not the fault of individuals, but a symptom of the superficial mindset of modern commercial society. Clearly, even though Defoe's critique of commercial competition was originally inspired by historical developments in eighteenth-century Britain, his insight into the moral emptiness of material ambition remains relevant in the present day.

Master List of Characters

Moll Flanders—*the main character and narrator of the novel; Nicknamed Moll Flanders by her confederates in crime, she spends her life striving to escape from poverty and servitude. After a series of brief and unfortunate marriages, Moll becomes one of the most famous and successful criminals in England.*

Moll's Mother— *After giving birth to Moll in Newgate Prison, Moll's mother, a petty thief, is transported to the colonies. She and Moll are reunited many years later when Moll travels to America.*

The Nurse—*a kind and hard-working seamstress and teacher; Moll lives with the nurse from early childhood until age fourteen.*

The Elder Brother—*the eldest son in a wealthy family that takes Moll in during her adolescence; An irresponsible and dishonest character, the Elder Brother seduces Moll by preying on her pride and vanity.*

Robin—*the earnest younger son in Moll's wealthy "foster family"; Robin falls in love with Moll and asks her to marry him even though she is destitute. Although Moll is in love with his older brother, she accepts Robin's proposal. Robin dies five years into their marriage.*

The Draper—*Moll's second husband; A spendthrift gentleman, the Draper advises Moll to regard him as if he were dead and flees to France to escape from debt collectors.*

Moll's Brother—*Moll's third husband; Unaware of their blood relationship, Moll marries her brother, who takes her to Virginia to live on a plantation with his mother. When Moll realizes that her mother-in-law is actually her own mother, she leaves her brother-husband to return to England. Many years later, when she re-encounters her brother in America, he is too blind and demented to heed her return.*

Jemy—*Moll's fourth husband; While courting Moll, Jemy pretends that he is rich because he thinks that she is wealthy. Although both are surprised when they discover their mutual poverty, they truly love each other. Jemy spends a month with Moll, then heads off to Ireland, because he is in trouble with the law and hopes*

to make his fortune outside England. He and Moll are reunited
years later in Newgate Prison.

The Banker—*Moll's fifth husband; A quiet and sensible man, the Banker divorces his promiscuous wife in order to marry Moll. The marriage lasts five years until he sickens and dies after making a bad investment.*

The Gentleman of Bath—*a generous married man who provides for Moll, first as a friend, then as a lover; After living with Moll for six years, he becomes ill while visiting his wife's relatives. When he recovers, he ends his affair with Moll in order to save his marriage and his soul.*

The Governess—*a midwife, pawnbroker, and thief who takes care of Moll during one of her pregnancies and later helps her dispose of stolen goods; The Governess lives off the wickedness of others and pushes Moll to commit many crimes, but she also stands by her friend in times of trouble.*

Moll's Son—*Born of her marriage to her brother, Moll's son grows up in America and becomes a wealthy planter. When Moll is nearing old age, she and her loving son are reunited in Virginia.*

The Sea Captain's Lady—*After Moll takes refuge in the Mint, a part of London customarily designated as a refuge for debtors, she helps the Sea Captain's Lady secure a husband. The Sea Captain's Lady returns the favor by helping Moll to find an apparently wealthy suitor.*

The Baronet—*Moll spends a night on the town with the Baronet and, when he falls into a drunken stupor, she robs him. Later, after she manages to make him pay her to return his possessions, they carry on an affair for about a year.*

The Wealthy Matrons—*a group of women who give Moll work and clothes during her childhood.*

Summary of the Novel

Moll Flanders tells the story of a beautiful, smart, and self-interested woman who strives to escape the poverty and servitude dictated by the lowly circumstances of her birth. Despite a complete lack of material resources, Moll becomes determined at a very early age to transform herself into a "gentlewoman." She proceeds to acquire a level of education and refinement far beyond her social station and expertly exploits her skills, as well as her physical charms, to procure a series of husbands. The most shocking of all of Moll's many misalliances is her relationship with her third husband, with whom she lives with for a brief but happy period in Virginia until she learns that he is actually her brother.

None of Moll's many marriages fulfills her material ambitions. When her youth and beauty fade, she chooses the only other road to wealth she can discern, a life of crime. She soon becomes an expert in her new career and, as reports of her criminal exploits circulate throughout England, she is nicknamed 'Moll Flanders' by her underworld associates. This label understandably irritates her. 'Moll' was used to denote a female criminal, while 'Flanders' was associated both with Flemish cloth, a favorite target for thieves, and also with Flemish prostitutes, who were supposed at the time to be the best in the profession. Moll does not, however, supply the reader with any other name. Instead, she emphasizes that the number and gravity of the offenses she has committed make it impossible for her to reveal her true identity.

By taking cover under this alias and employing a variety of disguises, Moll manages to avoid arrest for many years. During this period, she associates mainly with her "governess," a midwife who had helped her through one of her many pregnancies. The governess turns out to be both a loyal friend and an excellent connection to buyers of stolen property. She not only helps Moll reap handsome profits from her crimes, she also alerts Moll when opportunities for thievery arise. With the aid of her cunning but faithful friend, Moll gradually becomes the richest and most notorious thief in England.

Moll eventually grows careless of her safety and, as she herself had predicted many times, she is captured and returned to the place of her birth, Newgate Prison. Consumed by fear of execution, she prays with a prison minister and seemingly repents for her sins. Thanks to the minister's intervention, Moll's death sentence is reduced to transportation to the colony of Virginia. Before her departure to America, Moll meets up again with her favorite

Introduction

husband, Jemy, a highway robber, and persuades him to join her on her journey.

In America, Moll finds her brother-husband, blind and demented, living with one of their sons. Because she hopes to get hold of a legacy left to her by her mother, Moll informs her son of the unnatural relationship which led to his birth. Moll's son is delighted to be reunited with his mother. After he secures her inheritance, he showers her with kindness and presents. Moll and Jemy soon become wealthy planters and, after spending several years in Maryland, they return to England to live out the rest of their lives in repentance and prosperity.

Estimated Reading Time

Reading *Moll Flanders* should take approximately ten hours. Because characters sometimes appear and disappear rather quickly within the novel, the best way to read the story is to make notes and compare them to summaries and analyses contained in this *MAXnotes* guide. *Moll Flanders* is not divided into separate chapters. The divisions defined in this guide are designed to maximize your understanding of the characters and the sequence of events. Study questions appear at the end of every section. You can rely on these, as well as the chapter summaries and analyses, to delineate the most significant themes and topics addressed in Defoe's work.

SECTION TWO

Moll Becomes a "Gentlewoman"

Preface

Summary

In his brief introduction, Defoe pretends that he is presenting the reader not with a work of fiction, but with a somewhat sanitized version of Moll Flanders' memoirs of her life of crime. While acknowledging that many aspects of Moll's history are lewd and vulgar, Defoe contends that he could not purge the manuscript of these defects without damaging the authenticity of her story. He accordingly apologizes for placing so many sordid and immoral incidents before the public. However, he emphasizes that, while he did his best to clean up the offensive language Moll herself employed when she wrote down her recollections, he was driven to leave in many indecent details, not by any will of his own, but by his sacred commitment to truth.

Analysis

The highly ironic stance Defoe takes in his short introduction sets the tone for the entire work. By protesting too vigorously against those who might mistake the book for a piece of immoral entertainment, he emphasizes that it is racy enough to excite the lowest desires. Thus, by strongly condemning anyone who might derive some depraved pleasure from Moll's sordid history, he effectively invites people to read her story for precisely that reason.

Part One: Moll's Early Life

New Characters:

The Nurse: *the woman who cares for Moll during her childhood*

The Wealthy Matrons: *the rich women who help Moll during her childhood*

The Elder Brother: *the eldest son in a wealthy family that takes Moll in during her adolescence*

Robin: *the younger son in Moll's "foster family"*

Summary

Moll Flanders, the narrator of the novel, begins her revelation of her life history by stressing that "Moll Flanders" is not her real name, but a nickname invented by her criminal associates. Though she admits that there is no excuse for the terrible sins she has committed, she observes that her life of crime seemed almost predetermined by the circumstances of her birth in Newgate Prison, the most ghastly jail in all of England. Moll observes that her mother, a petty thief, was transported to the colonies a few months after giving birth, an event which allowed Moll to fall into the hands of gypsies until she somehow managed to escape when she was three years old.

Moll recalls being placed in the care of a poor but decent woman to whom she refers as "nurse." The nurse, who ran a school for local girls, not only taught Moll how to read and sew, she took great pains to make sure that Moll learned how to be polite and well-mannered. When Moll turned eight, the town authorities suggested that she be removed from her nurse's care and placed into household service. Utterly determined to avoid this fate, Moll attempted to convince her nurse to keep her by declaring that she would learn how to support herself by doing needlework. In making her case to the nurse, Moll declared that she would make enough money, not only to pay for her room and board, but to provide herself with the resources required to become a "gentlewoman."

Moll could not understand why her nurse and the wealthy

matrons of the town found her ambition to become a gentlewoman highly amusing. Whereas these women knew that true gentility required high birth and a substantial fortune, Moll believed that the term "gentlewoman" applied to any woman who earned enough money to avoid household service. The rich women of the town found Moll's aspirations so entertaining that they not only arranged for her to remain with her nurse, they also paid her generously for her needlework, gave her pretty clothes, and allowed her to associate with their own daughters. As she became a favorite among these women and acquainted with girls far above her social station, Moll became increasingly convinced that her superior beauty, charm, and manners would carry her to a lofty position.

Soon after Moll turned fourteen, her nurse died, leaving her, it seemed, to fend for herself sooner than she had expected. However, the Mayor's wife and a few other wealthy ladies were more than willing to take her in, not as a servant, much to Moll's relief, but as a companion to their children. Moll went to live with one of the richest families of the town, a household which, in addition to two relatively plain-looking daughters, also included two attractive sons. Although these people did not regard Moll as a member of their family, they treated her extremely well, supplied her with elegant clothes, and allowed her to remain present during their daughters' singing, dancing, language, and writing lessons. Thanks to this instruction, as well as her good manners and great beauty, Moll quickly distinguished herself as an extraordinarily attractive and accomplished young woman, an achievement which earned her the envy of the daughters in her foster family, as well as the steady admiration of both older sons.

Analysis

From the start of the novel, Defoe accentuates the main theme of Moll Flanders: moral ambiguity. For example, Moll is supposed to be relating her life history in order to teach readers that immoral acts never go unpunished. However, even while supposedly revealing this genuine moral principle, Moll refuses to provide her real name and thus continues to avoid prosecution for her crimes. At the same time, while speculating that she might have lived a purer life had she "not been left a poor desolate girl without friends,

without clothes, without help or helper," she admits that most of her misdeeds would never have occurred had she not been consumed by material ambition and bewitched by a tendency to think too well of herself.

Moll's determination to become a gentlewoman can be interpreted in at least two ways. On one hand, in view of the strict divisions between the rich and the poor in eighteenth century Britain, Moll's desire to rise above her social station can be viewed as an unnatural violation of custom and tradition and, therefore, defined as her fatal flaw. On the other hand, the idea that Moll should have done without social recognition and, despite her beauty, intelligence, and manners, simply resigned herself to her lowly position seems irrational and unfair. The conflicting explanations Moll provides for her vicious conduct at the beginning of the story are not resolved in the course of the story. On the contrary, Defoe prompts readers to speculate about Moll's blameworthiness throughout the book.

Part Two: "The Ordeal of Virtue"

Summary

By the time Moll turned eighteen, both sons were smitten by her great beauty. The elder son, a handsome and irresponsible young man, frequently arranged to be alone with Moll and, whenever his schemes succeeded, he showered her with compliments, caresses, and presents. Though Moll describes her character at this period as that of a "very sober, modest, and virtuous young woman," she admits that she willingly allowed this young man to take advantage of her need for attention and pleasure. Indeed, she emphasizes that the elder son could have robbed her of virtue with much less effort.

One day, the elder son devised an elaborate plan to meet Moll alone at the house of a friend. As soon as the couple arrived at his friend's empty house, the elder brother professed his love for Moll and promised to marry her as soon as he came into his fortune. This vow, along with a purse full of gold, was sufficient to remove the last remnant of Moll's resistance. After the older brother had his way with Moll and both arrived back at home without arousing suspicion, they proceeded to repeat their wickedness at every opportunity. Though Moll frequently regretted the sinful state into which she had fallen, she silenced her conscience by reminding herself of the elder brother's talk of marriage, by focusing on all the money he gave her, and by luxuriating in the pleasure she derived from his frequent compliments.

Moll and the elder brother carried on their affair for over six months, but no one ever discovered them together or detected the true nature of their relationship. Meanwhile, Robin, the younger son in Moll's 'foster family,' became so enamoured of her that he began to broadcast his admiration not only to her, but to his parents and sisters. While the other members of the family clearly disapproved of Robin's love for Moll, his elder brother began to realize that Robin could provide him with an escape from the promises he had made in order to win her affection. Upon hearing that Robin had formally offered to marry Moll, the elder brother did his best to convince his lover to accept his brother's proposal.

Moll was extremely shocked to learn that the elder brother hoped she would marry Robin. In the course of their affair, she had become convinced that her love for him was genuine, and she had also rationalized their intimacy on the grounds that he would one day become her husband. However, when she realized that the elder brother would never risk his inheritance by marrying a destitute woman, Moll concluded that she had no choice but to accede to Robin's request. Consequently, after the elder brother bribed with five hundred pounds, Moll married Robin even though she "had not the least affection" for him.

Robin's devotion to Moll never inspired her to return his love. While she admits that Robin always treated her with great respect and admiration, she declares, "I never was in bed with my husband but I wished myself in the arms of his brother." Moll did not have to carry on her false relationship with Robin for very long. Five years into their marriage, he suddenly sickened and died, leaving her with little more than what she had been able to save of the money given to her by the elder brother during and after their affair. Given her limited resources, Moll decided that the most practical course of action was to find a wealthy husband without delay.

Analysis

Moll's calculating and mercenary approach to relationships shows itself throughout this section of the novel. Of the money the elder brother gave her to win her affection, she remembers that she "told," that is, counted the coins, "over a thousand times a day." "Later, she consented to Robin's proposal only because she realized that she would never be able to marry his elder brother and only after the elder brother bribed her with five hundred pounds. Moreover, even after she married Robin, she made no effort to forget his older brother. Instead, she made a mockery of her marriage by dreaming of her former lover whenever she found herself in her husband's arms. Thus, rather than repenting of her sins, Moll reasoned that her virtue had been lost forever and, having resigned herself to the role of a 'fallen' woman, concluded that she might as well give herself over to material comfort and pleasure while travelling down the road to eternal damnation.

Thanks to her utterly materialistic view of social relationships, Moll has been characterized as the personification of eighteenth–century capitalism. Her insatiable appetites and her shrewd attempts to gain as much as possible from every situation indicate that Defoe's purpose in this novel was, at least in part, to illustrate the corrupting effects of the passion for private gain. Like many members of the social elite in this period, Moll talks a great deal about moral questions, but her only discernable motivation in nearly every situation is limitless greed. Thus, Moll's self-serving rationalizations of her actions express one of the most troubling questions raised by the rise of capitalism in eighteenth–century Britain, that is, does the universal pursuit of economic self-interest deprive individuals of the capacity to comprehend the moral consequences of their behavior?

Study Questions

1. Where was Moll born?
2. What happened to Moll's mother?
3. How does Moll spend the first three years of her life?
4. Where does Moll live during most of her childhood?

5. What was Moll's driving ambition while she was growing up?
6. What does Moll identify as her worst failing?
7. What impressed Moll most during her affair with the elder brother?
8. Why did Moll marry Robin, her first husband?
9. How long were Moll and Robin married?
10. What happened to the children Moll had with Robin?

Answers

1. Moll was born in Newgate Prison in London, England.
2. Moll's mother was sentenced to death by hanging after being convicted for petty theft. However, after she 'pled her belly,' that is, let prison authorities know that she was pregnant, her sentence was reduced to transportation to the American colonies.
3. After Moll's mother was shipped off to the colonies, Moll was taken by gypsies from Newgate Prison. She traveled about with them until she somehow managed to escape when she was three years old.
4. Moll lived with a school mistress to whom she refers as 'nurse.' The nurse cared for Moll until she was fourteen years old.
5. Moll wished to become an independent "gentlewoman."
6. Moll names vanity as her downfall.
7. Moll enjoyed the money and physical pleasure the elder brother gave her.
8. The elder brother made it clear that he would never marry Moll, and he also bribed her with five hundred pounds.
9. Robin and Moll were married for five years.
10. According to Moll, "the two children were indeed taken happily off my hands by my husband's father and mother."

Part Two

Suggested Essay Topics

1. Discuss the significance of the fact that Moll was born in Newgate Prison. After summarizing the details Moll provides about the jail, describe what an individual who was born there during this era might expect to accomplish in life.
2. Explore Moll's ambition to become a "gentlewoman." Explain Moll's misunderstanding of this term and describe how the wealthy matrons of the town responded to Moll's aspirations.

SECTION THREE

Moll's Early Adventures in Marriage

Part Three: The Draper

New Characters:

The Draper: *Moll's second husband*

The Linen Draper: *Moll's landlord after the death of her first husband*

The Linen Draper's sister: *the woman who introduces Moll to her second husband*

Summary

Vowing to find a rich husband before her savings ran out, Moll took a room in the home of a linen-draper. She soon discovered that the linen-draper desired her to become his mistress, but she decided to hold out for a man who would take her as his wife. Moll turned to the linen-draper's sister, a somewhat dissolute woman of wide acquaintance, to help her locate a suitable catch. The linen-draper's sister introduced Moll to a variety of men. However, none of the likeable ones seemed to be interested in marriage, while none of the marrying kind appeared at all appealing.

Part Three

After many disappointments, Moll finally encountered the type of man she had been seeking, another draper, but a "gentleman-tradesman" who seemed to have the wherewithal both to provide her with material comforts and to keep her entertained. Moll never lied to the gentleman-tradesman about her financial circumstances, but she managed to give him a highly exaggerated impression of her material worth. Meanwhile, in view of his lavish lifestyle, she surmised that he possessed a considerable fortune. Because she believed that he would soon begin to draw from his own bank accounts, Moll allowed him to spend a great deal of her money during the first months of their marriage.

As time passed, Moll began to realize not only that her husband had less money than she did, but that his spending habits were entirely out of control. When her husband was arrested for debt and confined to a "sponging house," a debtors' prison, Moll was distressed, but not surprised. Moll's husband sent for her to meet with him in prison and instructed her to gather as many of his valuables as she could lay her hands on and place them somewhere safe from debt collectors. He also told her that his predicament obliged him to abandon her and flee to France.

Moll followed her husband's directives and, a few weeks later, received a letter from him from France telling her how to redeem certain items he had deposited with pawnbrokers. Although Moll made a significant profit from the sale of these goods, she worried about her prospects in life. She knew her husband would never return, but the fact that he was still alive and still her husband meant that she could not marry again without violating the law or without lying about her situation. To give herself time to contemplate her next move, Moll took rooms in a section of London known as the Mint, a part of town that served as a customary haven for fugitives and debtors.

During this period, Moll posed as a widow and, for a time, called herself "Mrs. Flanders." Although she was repulsed by the low characters she encountered in the Mint, she appreciated the anonymity she gained by taking shelter there. She accordingly decided to leave as soon as she managed to put her affairs in order and find a better place.

Analysis

When Robin died, Moll grieved not about his demise, but about her economic circumstances, a response that confirms her purely materialistic approach to marriage. In her usual style, she admits that she "was not suitably affected by the loss of my husband;" then, rather than resolving to improve her behavior, moved on to an even more demoralized relationship with the draper. What made the draper particularly attractive, Moll recalls, was that he came into a sum of money which, combined with her savings, enabled them to travel about the country with an entourage of servants. Thus, Moll observes, "I was hurried on by my fancy to a gentleman, to ruin myself in the grossest manner that ever woman did."

In line with her clear-eyed resignation to her own shortcomings, Moll never blames the draper for misleading her about the size of his fortune. On the contrary, she acknowledges that she frittered away their money as carelessly as he did. After he flees to France and she ends up living in isolated obscurity among the debtors and scoundrels in the Mint, she concedes that her situation was much better than any woman who had misbehaved as she did had any right to expect. The sympathetic aspects of Moll's character are thus contradicted by her endless attempts to evade the destiny she seems to deserve.

Moll's stay in the Mint adds an interesting historical dimension to the narrative. During this period of British history, modern conceptions of private property were being gradually introduced into the legal system. While these laws remained in flux, petty thieves and debtors retained some access to places such as the Mint. These havens were generally located near prisons and customarily served as a sort of grey zone between freedom and incarceration. Those who took refuge in such places were understood to have violated the law in some way, either by committing crimes against property or by refusing to pay their debts. Some of the inhabitants of these areas avoided imprisonment by paying persons in authority to put off prosecution of their cases, while others (like Moll) took advantage of the obscurity attached to living in such a place. Although movement in and out of these areas was supposed to be somewhat restricted, Moll's easy attitude about leaving the Mint illustrates that the rules governing these places were vague and rarely enforced.

Part Four: An Unnatural Alliance

New Characters:

The Widow: *Moll's landlady after she moves to the Mint*

The Sea Captain's wife: *A friend Moll helps to snare a husband*

The Sea Captain: *The husband of Moll's newest friend*

Moll's Third Husband: *A relatively wealthy man who owns land in Virginia*

Moll's third husband's mother: *a former criminal who lives on her son's estate in the colony of Virginia*

Summary

Soon after her removal to the Mint, Moll realized that she would never find the type of husband she desired among the ruffians who filled the taverns and gaming houses there. Consequently, when a widow offered her lodging in another part of town, Moll accepted right away.

During this period, Moll became friendly with a neighbor who was having trouble with a sea captain to whom she had been engaged. The sea captain had called off his engagement to Moll's neighbor after his fiancée tried to investigate his financial circumstances. In order to help her neighbor win the captain back, Moll persuaded her to spread false accounts of how much money he owed and to circulate rumors designed to blacken his reputation. Meanwhile, Moll's neighbor and Moll herself made all of their acquaintances believe that the captain's former fiancée was being courted by an extremely wealthy gentleman. Moll's scheme met with immediate success. The captain came back to his former fiancée, begged her to renew their engagement and, when she brought up all the questions which had lately been raised about his financial dealings, he provided her with a detailed report of his accounts.

The sea captain's bride was so grateful for Moll's assistance that she promised to return the favor by helping her friend make a similarly attractive match. First, the sea captain's wife convinced her husband that Moll was worth a fortune. Then, after the sea captain spread news of Moll's wealth throughout the neighborhood, a crowd of suitors lined up to win her hand. From the swarm of men around her, Moll chose a particularly attractive gentleman who collected considerable income from an estate he owned in the colony of Virginia.

Both before and after they were married, Moll told this gentleman that reports of her great fortune were inaccurate, but she never let him know exactly how much money she had. Initially, Moll's suitor thought she was merely being coy and that her talk was designed to make sure that he was not a fortune-hunter. A short time after they were married, however, Moll began to speak so freely of her meager resources that her husband began to fear that she was completely destitute. Thus, when she presented him with £600, the whole extent of her savings, he was grateful for the gift rather than angry that he had been mislead about her financial situation.

Moll's husband realized that he and Moll would have to live on much less than he had expected and therefore suggested that they move from England to Virginia so that he could maximize his income from his land. After a long and harrowing trip across the ocean, which included an encounter with pirates, Moll and her husband arrived in Virginia where they were welcomed by his mother. From that point, all three lived together on his plantation.

While her husband was out tending to his business affairs, Moll spent countless hours talking with his mother, who, it turned out, had lived a highly colorful and adventurous life. For several years, Moll was perfectly happy in America, helping her husband as much as she could and taking pleasure in his mother's entertaining tales. One day, however, while listening to her husband's mother describe the circumstances which had brought her to Virginia decades before, Moll made a horrifying discovery.

Moll's mother-in-law first observed that many of the leading inhabitants of the colony had arrived as convicts, but had risen to wealth and prominence after paying their debts to society. Then, in order to illustrate that she was not ashamed to be included in this company, the old woman took off her glove and showed Moll a brand that had been burned into her hand upon her conviction for theft. Moll's mother explained that, like most convicted felons at the time, she had been sentenced to death. However, because

Part Four 25

she was pregnant and very near to giving birth, prison officials reduced her sentence to several years of indentured servitude (forced labor) in the American colonies.

As she listened to her mother-in-law recall giving birth to a baby girl in Newgate Prison, Moll grew increasingly uneasy. Hearing all of the details of the story confirmed Moll's worst fear: the baby the old woman spoke of was Moll herself. Moll had therefore married her own half-brother and thus had unknowingly entered into an entirely unnatural and morally reprehensible relationship. Moll concealed her realization from her mother while she tried to determine what she ought to do. In the meantime, however, she recognized that she now "lived there in open avowed incest and whoredom," although she later acknowledges that she "was not much touched by the crime of it."

Determined to escape from her predicament, Moll eventually confessed her real identity to her mother and, throughout this period, did her best to avoid any intimacy with her husband-brother. Much to her daughter's surprise, Moll's mother advised her to pretend that the revelation of their true relationship had never come to pass. However, Moll could no longer bear the presence of her husband-brother. Consequently, in order to convince him to allow her to return to England, she finally informed him that they were brother and sister and, therefore, could not live as man and wife. This confession obliged him to consent to her departure, but the shock of the revelation seemed to drive him slightly mad. Thus, having spent eight years in the colonies, Moll gathered up her possessions to set sail back to England.

Analysis

This section of the novel focuses on Moll's increasingly hardened resignation to her false and immoral existence. Every misdeed she remembers seems to have pushed her further down the road to complete corruption. Having concluded, for example, that the departure of the draper left her no choice but to snare another husband through deception, she proceeded to persuade her friend the captain's lady to recapture her fiancée in the most conniving way. Moll had, in other words, sunk so low that she began to drag others down to the level of wickedness that she herself had reached.

Moll sometimes castigates herself for her past behavior, but

Part Four 27

more often blames society for encouraging both men and women to regard relations between the sexes in an entirely unethical manner. Along these lines, Moll observes that, "Men choose mistresses by the gust of their affection and it was requisite for a whore to be handsome," while "for a wife, no deformity would shock the fancy, no ill qualities the judgement; the money was the thing." Cynical arguments such as these allow Moll to dispel some regrets about her wrongdoing, but they provide her with no comfort when her schemes fall apart.

Moll's ever more fatalistic frame of mind raises questions about the extent to which she ought to be held responsible for her actions. For instance, the fact that Moll's mother advised her to ignore her unnatural relationship with her husband suggests that Moll's moral defects might have been transmitted at birth.

Moreover, when Moll discovered that she had unknowingly married her brother, she viewed this accidental development as inevitable punishment for her earlier misdeeds. At the same time, however, Moll stresses that whenever she was forced to choose between virtue and vice, she always tilted without too much prompting toward the latter, not because the virtuous path was all that difficult, but because viciousness offered her a more immediate and pleasurable reward.

Study Questions
1. What was Moll's reaction to Robin's death?
2. What attracted Moll to the draper?
3. Why did Moll part with the draper?
4. Where did Moll go to live after the draper left her?
5. Where was Moll's third husband's estate?
6. What did Moll's mother display as a sign of her past?
7. What did Moll's mother advise Moll to do after Moll revealed the true relationship between her husband and herself?
8. What was Moll's third husband's reaction to the news that he had married his own half-sister?
9. How many children did Moll have with her husband-brother?
10. Where did Moll go after she resolved to end her relationship with her husband-brother?

Answers
1. After Robin died, Moll resolved to find a rich husband right away.
2. Moll liked the draper because he lived lavishly, kept many servants, and drove a fancy coach.
3. Moll and the draper were forced to part when he was taken to debtor's prison. They said their final goodbyes just before he fled to France.

Part Four

4. After the draper left her, Moll went to live in the Mint, a customary haven for fugitives and debtors.
5. Moll's third husband's estate was located in the colony of Virginia.
6. Moll's mother showed her daughter the brand she had received after she had been convicted of petty theft. The brand had been burned into Moll's mother's hand while she was incarcerated in Newgate Prison.
7. After Moll's mother learned that Moll has married her own brother, Moll's mother advised her daughter to pretend that the revelation had never come to pass.
8. When Moll's husband discovered that he had married his own sister, he became mentally unbalanced.
9. Moll had three children with her fourth husband, the man who turned out to be her own half-brother.
10. After Moll left her husband-brother, she sailed back to England with as many possessions as her relatives would allow her to take.

Suggested Essay Topics

1. Discuss Moll's view of the draper. Explain why she did not mind his tendency to spend beyond his means.
2. Explore the relationship between Moll and her mother. Discuss Moll's mother's recommendation that Moll keep her true relationship with her husband to herself.
3. Examine Moll's misalliance with her husband-brother. Try to determine why Defoe would place this unnatural marriage among Moll's calendar of crimes.

SECTION FOUR

Moll's Later Adventures In and Out of Marriage

Part Five: A Sinful Affair

New Characters:
The Landlady: *a woman who keeps a boarding house at Bath*
The Gentleman of Bath: *a married man who takes care of Moll*

Summary

When Moll arrived back in England after a storm-tossed journey, she lost track of much of the cargo she had arranged to have delivered and, being forced to wait for it to arrive at its proper destination, she decided to spend some time in the resort town of Bath. In keeping with the highly social atmosphere of Bath, she met a great many fast-living people, but soon found herself spending too freely, a habit she likens to "bleeding to death." During the off-season, she managed to relocate to cheaper lodgings with a relatively respectable lady and, by letting go her maid and reducing expenses, she carved out a comfortable, though somewhat dull and lonely life.

A gentleman Moll had encountered during the previous season returned to rent lodgings in the same boarding house. Moll's

Part Five

landlady told her that the gentleman was married, but that his wife suffered from an incurable mental disturbance. Although the gentleman was as honest and respectable as could be, his wife's illness made him hunger for an agreeable companion, a woman, he soon made clear, exactly like Moll herself. The gentleman paid a great deal of attention to Moll, and they soon became intimate friends. However, even though they passed freely into one another's rooms, meeting at all hours of the day and night in various degrees of undress, the gentleman never attempted to elicit more from Moll than a friendly kiss.

The gentleman kept up his extremely decorous behavior toward Moll even after he started to provide her with significant financial support. Eventually, the two became so perfectly easy with one another that they decided to take a holiday together in the countryside. When they arrived at their destination, the inn at which they planned to stay had available only one room with two beds. Since Moll and the gentleman had been intimate for so long without impinging on his marriage vows, neither protested this arrangement. In fact, the gentleman had so much confidence in his ability to refrain from molesting Moll that he declared that he could lie with her all night without subjecting her to any untoward advances. Much to Moll's amazement, the gentleman slept in Moll's bed and behaved exactly as he had promised.

From then on, Moll and the gentleman frequently occupied the same bed and, each time, Moll wondered how he managed to keep his passion in check. Then, one night, after drinking more wine than usual at dinner, Moll let the gentleman know that, if he happened to be in a mood to take their intimacy further, she would not object. "Thus," Moll recalls, "the government of our virtue was broken, and I exchanged the place of friend for that unmusical harsh-sounding title of Whore...and the bars of virtue and conscience being thus removed, we had the less difficulty afterwards to struggle with."

Soon after they commenced their sexual affair, Moll became pregnant and worried that the gentleman would leave her to face her ordeal alone. However, the gentleman made sure that Moll was well taken care of throughout her pregnancy and, without running into any problems, she gave birth to a healthy baby boy. Having no

great store of maternal feelings, Moll placed her baby in the care of a servant and proceeded to enjoy, in her words, "what I might call the height of my prosperity." Moll knew that her position was less secure than if she had been the gentleman's wife, but she truly enjoyed his companionship, as well as the fact that he gave her money enough to set aside considerable savings.

Six years into his affair with Moll, the gentleman went off for a visit to his wife's relatives. Upon his arrival at their house, he became deathly ill. Moll worried when he failed to return on schedule and agonized when she learned from one of the servants in the house that the gentleman was not expected to recover. Weeks passed and, by sending several anonymous messages to

Part Five

the house, Moll learned that the gentleman had experienced a miraculous change for the better. Although she wrote to the gentleman several times over the following months, she never received an answer. Finally, she found out that immediately after he had regained his health, he had sent a letter to her at Bath, explaining that his brush with death had convinced him to end their sinful relationship.

Analysis

Moll's deliberate effort to turn her friendship with the gentleman of Bath into a sexual relationship belies her claim that her "vice came in always at the door of necessity." Indeed, her defense of her conduct with this man is remarkably weak. "It is true, and I have confessed it before," she admits, "that from the first hour I began to converse with him, I resolved to let him lie with me if he offered it, but it was because I wanted his help...and I knew of no other way of securing him than that." As usual, Moll acknowledges that the means she used to achieve her objectives are less than admirable, but she never questions those objectives themselves. She never considers, for instance, whether she might have been more virtuous if she had given up her quest for wealth and pleasure and earned a humble living by taking in needlework.

As shameless as Moll seems to be, however, Defoe makes it difficult to sum her up as a purely bad character. On one hand, due in part to her straightforward approach to bad behavior, Moll remains likeable even while confessing her many avoidable crimes. On the other hand, taken within the context of eighteenth century Britain, when crowds of 'new-moneyed' men were reaping unprecedented profits from financial capitalism, Moll's greed seems representative rather than reprehensible. Moll's sins might have been worse than those committed by most other people, but her relentless drive to get and stay ahead was, as the moralists of the day never tired of complaining, typical among the upper and middle classes in eighteenth–century British society.

Part Six: Jemy

New Characters:

The Lancashire woman: *the person who introduces Moll to her fourth husband*

Jemy: *Moll's fourth husband*

The Banker: *Moll's fifth husband*

Summary

The gentleman of Bath sent Moll a good deal of money along with his regrets, but Moll was filled with anxiety about her future. Looking back at her situation, she points out that, "when a woman is thus left desolate and void of counsel, she is just like a bag of money, or a jewel dropped by the side of a highway, which is a prey to the next comer." In an effort to relieve her insecurity, Moll arranged to reside with a Lancashire woman whom she had met some years before. Like many of Moll's acquaintances, the Lancashire woman had been led to believe that Moll was extremely wealthy. In light of this misimpression, the Lancashire woman promised to introduce Moll to her brother, a gentleman who, the woman insisted, was also fabulously rich.

Before she moved to the north, Moll met several times with a very considerate banker in London. The banker not only promised to keep Moll's investments and accounts in order, he also let her know that he found her extremely attractive. The banker did not hide the fact that he was married. He stressed, however, that his loose-living wife had run off with a scoundrel, and that he was thinking of obtaining a divorce. When Moll replied that divorce was the only solution for husbands who found themselves tied to promiscuous women, the banker suggested that he and Moll marry as soon as his divorce was finalized.

Moll found the banker's offer highly appealing, but did not give her answer right away. She looked forward to meeting the Lancashire woman's brother and, hoping to explore this inviting prospect without limiting her options, she angled for more time to weigh the banker's proposal. She accordingly informed the banker that she had to travel north, but assured him that she would

Part Six

remain in touch. Although she did not explicitly lie to the banker, she gave him the false impression that, as soon as she returned, she would marry him without delay.

For the next six months, Moll was courted by the Lancashire woman's apparently wealthy brother, Jemy. In view of Jemy's seemingly large fortune and lavish style of living, Moll forgot about the banker and married her more recent suitor, dazzled by his description of his grand estate, as well as his magnificent clothes. About two months after Moll and Jemy were married, however, both discovered that each had been deceived. Jemy was astounded to learn that Moll owned nothing like the fortune his sister had described, while Moll was even more shocked when her husband confessed that his estate was only a fiction he had invented to win her hand.

Although both concluded that their lack of money would force them to part, neither expressed any anger over the deception each had practiced. On the contrary, Jemy expressed nothing but affection for Moll, while Moll declared that she loved Jemy more than any man she had met before. Rather than separating right away, the couple spent a blissful month together. Then, for reasons he never fully explained, Jemy went off to make his fortune in Ireland, promising to send for her if and when he managed to achieve financial success.

Once again, Moll found herself alone, only this time her distress derived from genuine heartbreak. Rather than lamenting her condition, Moll recollected the offer she had received from the banker. Luckily, it turned out that the banker had spent the seven months she had spent with Jemy trying to get his divorce finalized. Because Moll had never let him know about her marriage to Jemy, the banker continued to view Moll as a virtuous alternative to his promiscuous wife. In his letters, he implored Moll to hurry back to London so that they could be married at the earliest possible date.

Analysis

Moll's behavior during this period in her life suggests that she had fallen so deeply into wickedness that she could no longer comprehend the difference between virtue and vice. Thus, when the banker first offered her an opportunity to become his wife, she rejected him in favor of a man who had nothing to recommend

Part Six 37

him but vague reports about his fortune. Likewise, when she explains what led her to marry Jemy, she mentions nothing about his personal qualities; instead, she recollects his sister's talk about the size of his estate and remembers his splendid clothes. Moreover, Moll remained in love with Jemy even though he admitted that he deliberately deceived her, and he never provided her with a clear account of his history or his business affairs. Moll had by this point clearly become a creature of her likes and dislikes, less and less bothered, much less distressed, by any serious moral concerns.

Moll's conviction that dishonesty is always the best policy is evident in the fact that she carried on her correspondence with the banker even while professing her love for Jemy. In addition, her attachment to Jemy was apparently not sufficient to move her to tell him of the details of her life or even to inform him of her true identity. Thus, for Moll, true love is combined with resignation to falsity and, as a result, it no longer occurs to her that integrity might be an important factor to consider in the measurement of a husband.

The hardening of Moll's character over the course of her life saves Defoe's novel from its otherwise episodic quality. While the series of incidents described in the story sometimes seems rather loosely strung together, the change Moll undergoes in the course of her narrative defines the structure of the novel as a whole. Rather than merely confronting a variety of situations, Moll's experiences transform her relationships with others, as well as her conception of herself.

Part Seven: The Governess and the Banker

New Character:

The Governess: *a midwife who takes care of Moll during the birth of Jemy's child*

Summary

Having bid farewell to Jemy, Moll moved to London in order to resume her relationship with the banker. However, her discovery that

Part Seven

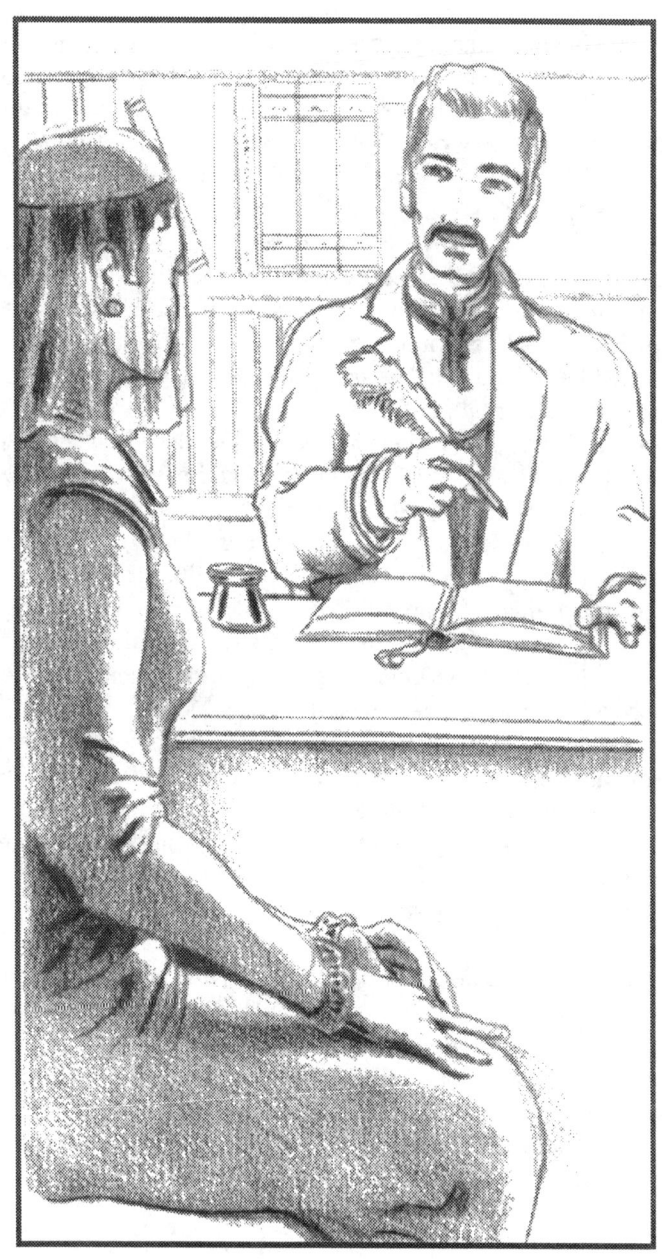

she was pregnant once again thwarted her plans. Fortunately, the banker's divorce remained unsettled, so Moll had several months to figure out how to handle her condition. When Moll's pregnancy became more apparent, Moll's landlady introduced her to a midwife who understood, not only the complexities of childbirth, but also the difficulties faced by women in Moll's solitary situation.

The "governess," as Moll called the midwife, had apparently gained her expertise by sheltering prostitutes and other outcast women. Moll was at first reluctant to identify herself as the type of individual who would require such assistance, but after the governess provided her with a detailed account of what she usually charged her clients, Moll recognized that she would be getting a real bargain. Consequently, Moll set aside her qualms about the governess's low connections and, after she placed herself in the midwife's care, her new friend's hospitality, dexterity, and wisdom convinced her that she had made exactly the right decision.

Soon after Moll gave birth to another healthy baby boy, she received a letter from the banker informing her that he was entirely free to marry because his wife had committed suicide. Moll was anxious to make good her promise to marry the banker, but she worried over the fate of her new child. After much debate with the governess, whom she had come to call "Mother," Moll decided to pay a country woman ten pounds to take the boy off her hands. Remembering her parting with the child inspires Moll to launch into a long discourse on maternal responsibility. In fact, Moll becomes so entranced by her reflections on how hard it was to break the sacred obligations of motherhood that she seems to forget that she had broken that trust before.

A few months after she gave away her child, Moll arranged to meet with the banker, making sure that their reunion would not provide him with any information about her previous whereabouts. As soon as they met, the banker insisted that they stop at an inn so that Moll could recover from her journey. Once they arrived, the banker tried to persuade Moll to marry him that very day. The banker's tender declarations of love inflamed Moll's guilty conscience. Stepping out of her usual rationalizations, she silently reproached herself:

> What an abominable creature am I! and how is this innocent gentleman going to be abused by me! How little does he think, that having divorced a whore, he is throwing himself into the arms of another...one that has lain with two brothers, and had three children by her brother! One that was born in Newgate, whose mother was a whore, and is now a transported thief; one that has lain with thirteen men, and has had a child since he saw me! Poor gentleman!

Moll's self-examination did not make her hesitate long. Vowing to repent of her transgressions and become a dutiful wife, she married the banker that night in a private ceremony at the inn.

The next morning, Moll happened to look out a window and was shocked to see Jemy, her Lancashire husband, and two companions ride up to an inn across the road. Moll carefully concealed her consternation from the banker, but did her best to convince him that they should find another place to stay. Several hours later, a noisy crowd gathered in the street in response to news that three highway men had robbed two coaches and some travellers not too far away. When witnesses identified Jemy and his companions as likely suspects, Moll assured the constable who was conducting the investigation that at least one of the men in question was a person of high social standing and great honesty. She also declared that all three had driven off another way. The constable accepted Moll's account and decided to search for another group of men. A few days later, when the banker determined that the roads were safe to travel, he and Moll set off to his home in London.

Though Moll had been shaken by the sight of Jemy, she felt extremely happy in her position as the banker's wife. Sharing his quiet way of living and enjoying his thoughtful protection convinced her that she had, in her words, "landed in a safe harbor, after the stormy voyage of life past was at an end." After five years of complete tranquillity, however, the banker lost a great deal of money in a foolish transaction. Moll tried to persuade him that their fortune could be recovered, but the banker could not put his loss behind him. He grew increasingly despondent and gradually wasted away from depression. Thus, upon the death of yet another husband, Moll found herself alone in the world again.

Analysis

Moll's experiences during this segment of the novel raise questions about where she belongs in the hierarchy of eighteenth-century British society. When she sought the assistance of the governess with the birth of Jemy's child, she contrasted with the midwife's usual clientele to the extent that she occupied a somewhat higher social station and had not, technically speaking, worked as a prostitute. However, she got along so well with the governess that she began to call her "mother," a term of endearment which suggests that Moll had arrived at a social position precisely suited to a person who had been born in Newgate Prison.

Moreover, just before Moll married the banker, she recognized how unfair it was for her to take advantage of his love and protection. Then, as if she were touched, as she puts it, by the "invisible hand" of destiny, she re-encountered Jemy the morning after the wedding. Just as she was about to enter what might have been the calmest and, from a moral standpoint, most promising of her many relationships, Jemy's reappearance forced her to actively mislead her husband and to lie to the authorities in order to throw them off the trail of her former lover. The message Defoe seems to be sending in these chapters is that Moll simply cannot rise above her sordid past.

It is also important to note that money plays an especially prominent role throughout this part of the narrative. Defoe not only emphasizes that Moll accepted the governess's help because of the low cost of her services, he provides the reader with a detailed rendition of her bill. Likewise, what is significant about Moll's relationship to the banker is not simply that he made his living by arranging and supervising financial transactions, but that a bad investment sent him to his death. Thus, in the course of the story, moral concerns are increasingly displaced by economic considerations. These aspects of Moll's autobiography clearly illustrate that the novel was designed as a comment on the commercialization of social relations in eighteenth–century Britain.

Study Questions

1. What distinguished Moll's affair with the gentleman of Bath from her previous relationships?

Part Seven 43

2. How did Moll view her relationship with the gentleman of Bath?
3. How did Moll meet Jemy, her fourth husband?
4. What distinguished Moll's relationship with Jemy from her previous relationships?
5. Why did Jemy leave Moll?
6. What did Moll do after Jemy left her?
7. What convinced Moll to place herself in the care of the governess?
8. How does Moll describe her efforts to manipulate the banker?
9. How many children did Moll have with the banker?
10. How old was Moll when the banker died?

Answers

1. Moll carried on her relationship with the gentleman of Bath even though she knew that he would never take her as his wife.
2. During her affair with the gentleman of Bath, Moll thought of herself as a 'whore,' but she enjoyed the money and security he provided her.
3. Moll was introduced to Jemy, her fourth husband, by a Lancashire woman who made Moll believe that Jemy was a wealthy aristocrat.
4. In contrast to her feelings about her previous husbands, Moll loved Jemy more than any man she had ever met before.
5. Moll and Jemy parted when he went off to make his fortune in Ireland.
6. After Jemy left her, Moll resolved to renew her relationship with the banker.
7. Moll placed herself in the governess's care after the governess presented her with a detailed "bill of fare." Although she

was somewhat hesitant to rely on a woman who made a living assisting prostitutes, Moll realized that the governess was ideally suited to help her deal with her 'delicate' situation.
8. Of her dealings with the banker, Moll recalls, "I played with this lover as an angler does a trout."
9. Moll and the banker had two children.
10. When the banker died, Moll was forty-eight years old.

Suggested Essay Topics

1. Examine the role of money in *Moll Flanders*. Trace Moll's obsession with money from the pleasure she received from the coins the elder brother gave her to her appreciation of the way the banker handled her accounts.
2. Explore Moll's view of motherhood. Be sure to note the way she seems to lose track of exactly how many children she has had.

Part Seven

SECTION FIVE

Adventures in Crime

Part Eight: Early Success

Summary

After the banker died, Moll sold most of her possessions and took rooms in a cheap boarding house. She managed to live there for about a year by stretching out her savings, but she came perilously close to complete impoverishment. In her misery, she took to reciting a prayer, "Give me not poverty lest I steal." Despite her appeals to God, she was soon subjected to a temptation that she found impossible to resist.

While wandering around the city, she passed a shop and spied a white bundle lying on a stool. Realizing that nobody in the shop was watching, she snatched the bundle without attracting notice from any of the clerks. After she arrived home and found that she had gotten away with some fine cloths, six silver spoons, a silver mug, and three silk handkerchiefs, as well as a small bag of coins and paper money, she shrank back in horror at the gravity of her crime. However, when she compared her conduct to the specter of starvation, she admitted that her sense of repentance would probably not last very long.

Some time later, Moll encountered a pretty little girl outside a dancing school. After speaking to the child in a friendly way, Moll took her by the hand and led her into a narrow alley. Then, pretending that she was adjusting the girl's clothes, Moll removed a string of gold beads from the child's neck. Moll recognized that robbing a

Part Eight 47

child should have inspired her to castigate herself for stooping so low, but the prospect of her own poverty deadened her conscience and hardened her heart.

Thanks to the many opportunities that came her way, Moll quickly developed her talents as a thief. One day, just as night was falling, a man bolted by her and threw a bundle into an alley near where she was standing. A few moments later, a small crowd of men also ran by, some of whom were yelling and shouting, "Stop

Thief!" When Moll saw that the men had captured the fugitive and were dragging him away, she stood by and waited for the crowd to pass. All she had to do at that point was to pick up the bundle and walk away. Looking over the expensive collection of goods she had netted, she congratulated herself for taking advantage of a particularly discriminating robber. Though adventures such as these always made her worry that she might be arrested, her early success convinced her that she had chosen exactly the right career.

Analysis

Moll's evaluation of her criminal endeavors parallels her thoughts about her sexual exploits. Just as she admits that she might have avoided losing her virtue, cheating her lovers, and lying to her husbands if she had managed to muster more inner strength, she acknowledges that she took to stealing before absolute necessity had actually arrived at her door. When she was seduced by the elder brother, for instance, she confesses that she never truly tried to resist his advances. Likewise, she became a robber, not when she was starving, but when an opportunity to steal presented itself.

Moll was, moreover, just as proud of her talent for stealing as she was vain about her ability to manipulate men. Her earlier contention that she had handled the banker just like "an angler does a trout" is mirrored in the way she congratulates herself every time she pulls off a clever or lucrative crime. These expressions of vanity illuminate one of the most indefensible aspects of Moll's character: even when her misdeeds get her into trouble, they bring her positive pleasure. Thus, in line with the ambiguous tone of the entire novel, the gratification Moll derives from doing evil makes it hard to accept at face value Defoe's assertion that his book was designed to show that crime does not pay. In Moll's case, crime turned out to be a fairly consistent source of both psychological satisfaction and economic gain.

Part Nine: Close Calls

Summary

As Moll became an increasingly busy thief, she built up a stockpile of stolen property that obliged her to find someone to help her find a market for her ill-gotten goods. Fortunately, she had remained in touch with the governess, the midwife who had helped her through the birth of Jemy's child. Moll visited the governess and found that the old woman was much poorer than she had been before, but still managed to make a meager living performing exactly the service Moll needed: fencing stolen goods. Without letting her old friend know how she had come by her possessions, she gave the governess several expensive items to sell.

Because the governess found customers willing to pay high prices for Moll's property, Moll came away from the transaction with a sum of money sufficient to set her mind somewhat at ease. In the meantime, having become too afraid of capture to remain at her old lodgings, Moll asked the governess if she could stay at her house while looking for a better way to earn her keep. After she relocated to her new home, Moll began to look for honest employment and, for the first time in decades, she took in sewing and needlework.

Moll vowed to do her best to refrain from stealing, but soon the "diligent devil" commanded her to return to her evil ways. One night, having stopped at a tavern for pint of ale, Moll stole a silver tankard and brought it back to the governess' house. Moll at first pretended that she had not meant to steal the tankard and told the governess that she planned to return it to its rightful place. If Moll did as she planned, the governess protested, she would undoubtedly be taken to prison and, like most thieves at that time, condemned to death. The governess advised Moll to be glad to have gotten away with the tankard, then went so far as to suggest that their life together would be much improved if Moll could "light on such a bargain once a week."

Upon hearing the old woman's positive reaction to the theft, Moll realized that her old friend was more involved in criminal activities than she had ever suspected. The governess proceeded to tell Moll how she melted down a stolen plate so that its origin

Part Nine

could never be detected. Later, after she had melted Moll's tankard and given her the full value in order to teach her how much could be gained from stealing such things, the governess promised to help Moll become a truly expert thief. The governess introduced Moll to a highly accomplished robber who taught Moll how to make off with wallets and watches, how to snatch purses, and, most important of all, how to choose the perfect victim. When, not long after they met, Moll's mentor was caught shoplifting and taken to Newgate, Moll learned a lesson in caution. However, even after her teacher was hanged and many more of her comrades came to terrible ends, Moll continued to ply her trade.

Because Moll always seemed to know how to take maximum advantage of every opportunity, she reaped tremendous profits from her crimes. Once, for example, she managed to steal most of the prized possessions of an entire family by rushing in at exactly the right moment while their house was burning down. Another time she realized that she could make a great deal of money by alerting customs officials to a hiding place for smuggled goods. Although the deal required her to bargain with officials who would have arrested her immediately if they had discovered her true identity, the profits she and the governess reaped from this transaction seemed to eclipse the risk involved.

Moll's intelligence usually saved her even when her accomplices were captured, but she endured many close calls. One day, for example, she tried to snatch a watch from a woman in a crowd and found that it was fastened too tightly. To distract the woman, Moll cried out as if she had been injured. At that moment, the woman screamed that someone had tried to pick her pocket. Then, just as Moll was bracing for certain arrest, another pickpocket in the crowd was caught red-handed. Since this fellow held a lady's watch, Moll's victim concluded that her attacker had been apprehended. Despite this turn of events, Moll still might have been detected, but because she was extremely well-dressed and wore a gold watch herself, she was able to ward off suspicion by pretending that she herself had very nearly been robbed.

In addition to dressing in fine clothes, Moll adopted a variety of disguises that saved her from arrest. Once, when the governess arranged for her to undertake a series of thefts with a young male accomplice, she disguised herself so cleverly that her accomplice believed she was a man. At the end of their spree, after her partner was captured, a crowd of witnesses to their most recent heist chased Moll into the governess's house, but because she shed her man's costume, and they had no reason to suspect that they had been pursuing a woman, the leaders of the crowd ended up apologizing to Moll and the governess for disturbing their home.

Analysis

In her recollections of her life of crime, Moll alternates between self-serving rationalizations and explicit admissions of guilt. When she robbed the little girl, she tried at first to excuse her crime by pointing out that the child should not have been left alone and should not have been wearing such an expensive necklace. She also pretended from time to time that she would never have been driven to commit such deeds had anyone taken pity on her and rescued her from poverty. In the end, however, she acknowledges that her heart had been hardened, not by the prospect of poverty, but by immediate material success.

While Moll is at least sometimes willing to lay the blame for her sins on herself, Defoe keeps the reader guessing about whether or not she deliberately chose to commit so many crimes. Moll's repeated remarks that she felt as if she had been possessed by the devil, and she often uses words such as "inevitable" to describe her behavior. Moll was also pushed to the height of her career by the governess, a woman who, in keeping with that title, should have been teaching her right from wrong and protecting her from harm. Moll herself might, in other words, have some reason to believe that she herself was a victim, corrupted from the moment of her birth.

This reading of Moll's character falls into line with the remarkably harsh punishments meted out for even the most petty crimes in eighteenth century Britain. During Defoe's lifetime, laws were passed to make many minor offenses punishable by death. Under these new laws, a thief might be sentenced to hang for filching a piece of cloth or stealing a spoon. Moll's descent into crime seems somewhat understandable in light of this system. Like those who enforced the law in her day, Moll placed all of her crimes on the same level and, once she had taken the initial step toward self-destruction with her first criminal act, nothing prevented her from going all the way. Since she was bound to receive the same penalty if she were caught stealing a handkerchief as she would if she were apprehended for stealing a purse of gold, Moll decided to try to get away with as many crimes as possible for as long as she could. Like many criminals during this period of British history, Moll continued stealing, not only because she had scarcely any way to make an honest living, but also because she had concluded that, sooner or later, she was bound to be hanged.

Part Ten: Captured

New Character:
The Baronet: *a man Moll robs who later becomes her lover*

Summary

Having escaped arrest for many years, Moll became, as her governess often said, "the richest of her trade in all of England." Perhaps as a result of her repeated triumphs, Moll grew increasingly restless and, like the stock brokers and investors who were also striking it rich in contemporary England, she looked for opportunities to diversify. One such opportunity came up when Moll visited a gambling parlor in a far off part of town. A drunken gentleman took notice of Moll and, after paying her compliments and presenting her with a portion of his winnings, he asked her to take a walk with him outside. The two spent some time walking in the streets and in some gardens, then the gentleman invited her to take a ride in his coach.

During their time together, the gentleman seemed to take Moll for a woman of a much younger age, a misimpression which might have been due to the fact that he never left off drinking. Despite his intoxication, the gentleman treated Moll very nicely. Consequently, when he stopped the coach and invited her into a house, she had no fears about going inside. Once they were alone in a room, however, he began to make advances and, falling back to the patterns of her younger days, Moll resisted at first and then gave in.

Afterwards, the gentleman and Moll returned to his coach, but soon after they drove off, the gentleman, who had never stopped drinking, fell fast asleep. Moll took the opportunity to relieve him of all of his possessions. Then, when his coach stopped to let another coach go by, Moll jumped out without attracting the driver's attention. Moll, as usual, excused the theft by blaming the gentleman for making himself such an easy target. Likewise, she reasoned that he probably had a virtuous wife at home and, in light of his thoughtless view of marriage, undoubtedly deserved to suffer for his faithless behavior.

Moll's governess was especially delighted with Moll's caper because she knew a way to make the gentleman pay dearly for the return of his goods. From the description Moll gave her of the gentleman, his coach, and the part of town they had visited, the governess guessed his identity and, the next day, found out where he lived. The governess proceeded to arrange a meeting with the gentleman, who turned out to be a baronet, in order to find out how much he would pay both to regain his property and to silence gossip about the night he had spent with Moll. As it turned out, the baronet was more than willing to pay for the governess' discretion and, having heard that Moll was not a prostitute but, in the words of her governess, "a gentlewoman," he asked to see her again.

On the night that she expected the baronet to visit, Moll dressed in her best clothes and, for the first time in her life, painted her face, a practice she had always rejected because she associated it with prostitutes. After Moll and the baronet spent the night together, he gave her a small sum of money as he was leaving. Although the transaction was, in a sense, more vulgar than any she had engaged in before, she comments only that, "it was the first money I had gained that way in years."

Although Moll hoped that the baronet would take her as his mistress and provide her with an alternative to stealing, his visits were sporadic and the money he gave was insufficient. Consequently, Moll continued to pursue her previous career. She eventually committed so many crimes that she began to steal out of sheer habit, even when there was no benefit to be gained. Her most irrational crime was set in motion when a man asked her to hold his horse while he went inside a tavern. Given a clear chance to walk away with another person's property, Moll led the horse back to the home of her governess. Of this folly, Moll admits, "never was a poor thief more at a loss to know what to do with anything that was stolen." Since neither she nor the governess had any use for the horse, they returned it to the tavern; finding it too risky to demand a ransom, neither derived any advantage from the whole affair.

Some of the other highlights of Moll's criminal endeavors included robbing wealthy families by pretending to have come to pick up sewing and stealing trunks at country inns when unsuspecting guests stepped out of their rooms. Moll also made money by eliciting false accusations from shopkeepers and then suing them for their mistakes. These activities led to dozens of near-arrests, but Moll never slackened her criminal pace. Even when the governess suggested that their fortune was so large that it made no sense to continue stealing, Moll gloried in the fact that her name had become more well-known than that of any thief who had ever spent time in Newgate or who had been tried in the Old Bailey, the court in which criminals were prosecuted after arrest.

Finally, however, when Moll failed to take proper care in a routine robbery at a linen shop, two women caught her and held her until a constable arrived. Moll pleaded to be let go and argued that, since she had returned the cloths she had taken, no one would profit by sending her to prison. All of Moll's begging fell on deaf ears. She was carried off to Newgate to be tried for stealing.

Analysis

The main theme in these chapters is Moll's almost complete loss of self-control. Her criminal activities, which might have been at first explained by fear of poverty, became an irresistible obsession. Rather than seeking security, Moll recklessly risked her safety, not because she had the slightest need for money, but because she gloried in her audacity and fame.

Moll's increasing irrationality is apparent not only in her theft of the horse, but also in her dealings with the baronet. She played the part of a prostitute, a role she had previously avoided, even though she had no reason to sink so low as to sell her body. Her attempts to earn money in this fashion seem not so much designed to increase her fortune as to see how far she could get beyond the bounds of morality. At this point, in other words, Moll began to look at crime as an end in itself.

Part Ten

Despite her self-congratulatory view of her crimes, Moll's behavior at the end of her criminal career suggests that she yearned for someone or something to save her from herself. She accordingly pursued her relationship with the baronet in the vague hope that his protection would prevent her from stealing. Indeed, Moll was so anxious to find some alternative to thievery that she was willing to place herself in the abject position of a prostitute. Likewise, her recklessness indicates that she longed to be caught. Given the sordid depths of Moll's behavior during this part of her life however, it seems that she hoped, not for moral redemption, but only to salvage some remnant of her individual identity.

Defoe does not go so far as to intimate that Moll had begun to lose her sanity, but her state of mind at this point of her life suggests that she had begun to suffer from serious bouts of irrationality. The moral of this segment of Moll's autobiography accordingly seems to be that, whatever criminals may gain from their activities, their efforts to transcend the common bounds of morality eventually cause them to lose their grip on reality. Thus, the deeper Moll descended into the criminal world, the more she suffered from fits of confusion. Ultimately, her entirely illegitimate efforts to achieve some degree of economic independence made her lose touch with her sense of self.

Study Questions

1. Why does Moll take up stealing?
2. What did Moll do when she moved into the governess' house?
3. Who was Moll's most significant partner in crime?
4. What was Moll's specialty as a thief?
5. Who does Moll blame most often for her misdeeds?
6. Who was the famous thief who taught Moll how to be a pickpocket?
7. Where did Moll meet the baronet?
8. What significant act did Moll perform while she was waiting to receive the baronet?

Part Ten

9. What was Moll's most irrational criminal act?
10. Where was Moll taken after she was captured?

Answers

1. Moll says that fear of starvation forced her to steal, but she admits that she engaged in criminal acts long before genuine poverty had arrived at her door. Indeed, Moll acknowledges greed as the most consistent inspiration for her crimes.
2. When Moll first moved in with the governess, she took in needlework, a sign that somewhere deep in her soul, she wished that she could make an honest living.
3. After Moll made it clear that she was willing to make a living by stealing, the governess became her most important partner in crime.
4. Even during the earliest stages of her career, Moll's specialized in stealing watches from ladies' sides.
5. Moll sometimes blames her victims for presenting themselves as easy targets, but more often says that the devil compelled her to break the law.
6. The beautiful and notorious 'Moll Cutpurse' taught Moll how to be an expert pickpocket, sharpening skills Moll had already developed to some degree on her own.
7. Moll met the baronet in a gambling house.
8. Moll painted her face like a prostitute before the baronet arrived.
9. Moll stole a horse even though neither she nor the governess had anything to gain from the act.
10. Moll was taken back to Newgate Prison, the place of her birth.

Suggested Essay Topics

1. Discuss the significance of Moll's relationship to the baronet. Try to explain why Moll would be eager to place herself in such a demoralized relationship.

2. Examine Moll's increasingly irrational approach to crime. List the indications that Moll wanted to be caught.

3. Examine the parallels between Moll's adventures in marriage and her adventures in crime. Discuss the personality traits Moll exhibits from early adolescence through late middle age.

Part Ten

SECTION SIX

Repentance and Prosperity

Part Eleven: Newgate Prison

New Character:

The minister: *a clergyman who visits Moll in prison and convinces her to repent*

Summary

When Moll first came to Newgate and found herself trapped in the noise, stench, filth, and gloom of the place, she was filled with terror. The complete disorder she encountered, along with the utterly depraved characters she saw drinking and playing cards in the wretched rooms, convinced her that she had truly descended into hell. Gradually, however, as she reflected on how long she had expected to be placed there and saw how many of the inmates had likewise been expecting her arrival, she began to adjust to her new home.

As horrible as Newgate was, Moll observes, time and experience taught the prisoners there to become so inured to the place that, "at last they become reconciled to that which at first was the greatest dead upon their spirits in the world, and are as impudently cheerful in their misery as they were when they were out of it." Moll likewise admits that she cannot comprehend "how hell should become by degrees so natural," but she remembers, nevertheless,

Part Eleven

that she began to find her situation, "not only tolerable, but even agreeable."

The routine Moll fell into so soon after she arrived in prison was suddenly interrupted when she caught sight of Jemy, her Lancashire husband, in the men's section of the common yard. From her fellow prisoners, she learned that Jemy and two other men had been taken to Newgate after a highway robbery. The three men were the objects of a great deal of awe and admiration among the inmate population, because they had reportedly valiantly resisted arrest. Moll could not speak with her former husband, but she inwardly begged his forgiveness for her role in advancing his life of crime. Jemy, she believed, would never had ended up in a place such as Newgate if the two had never met.

As the day of her trial approached, Moll regretted some of the harm she had caused to the people she loved, but she felt little remorse for her crimes. She did pray that she would be released from prison, but she concluded that the only way her prayers might be answered would be for the governess to bribe the jurymen who had been selected to decide her case. Unfortunately, the governess' efforts to convince the members of the jury to show Moll mercy proved unsuccessful. After spending several weeks waiting for her case to be heard, Moll was found guilty of thieving and sentenced to death.

The governess was so distressed by her inability to help Moll that she sought comfort from a minister and, with his encouragement, swore to remain an honest and upright Christian for the rest of her life. Then, hoping that her friend would also repent of her sins, she arranged for the minister to visit Moll in Newgate Prison. During her long meeting with the minister, as he spoke of the salvation of the souls of the wretched, Moll began to feel the first pangs of repentance. When he came to see her again, and filled her head with thoughts of divine mercy and infinite goodness, Moll felt a profound sense of shame for all of her sins and, at the same time, began to contemplate the benefits she might derive if she portrayed herself as a true penitent. The minister was so impressed by Moll's apparent repudiation of all her sins that he intervened with prison officials in an attempt to get her a reprieve. Thanks to his intercession, Moll's sentence was ultimately reduced from death to transportation to the American colonies.

Part Eleven

Analysis

Moll's relatively easy adjustment to life in Newgate can be construed as a sign that she had ended up exactly where she belonged. The fact that she not only felt comfortable among her fellow inmates, but also re-encountered Jemy, the only man she had ever loved, suggests that Newgate, the place of her birth, provided her for the first time with a kind of family. Likewise, having finally been captured, Moll was relieved of her deepest source of anxiety. From a psychological standpoint, prison offered Moll the ultimate refuge. No longer required to hide her real self or to lie to those around her, she had at last arrived in a place in which she could truly relax.

At the same time, the fact that Moll repeatedly likens Newgate to hell can be used to support the notion that her incarceration served as a symbolic prelude to her redemption. From this perspective, the time she spent between her capture and her apparent reformation can be read as a spiritual death, while the reduction of her sentence from hanging to transportation can be seen as a symbolic resurrection. Moll's reaction to seeing Jemy in Newgate lends some credence to this interpretation. Upon seeing him, Moll blamed herself for placing him on the path towards destruction. This was the first time in her long life that she ever took any responsibility for her actions. From this, it can be argued that, having returned to the place where she was born, Moll underwent a genuine spiritual rebirth.

As usual in *Moll Flanders*, certain aspects of the story contradict both of these interpretations. Thus, the fact that Moll connived to get out of prison belies the contention that Newgate can be viewed as her real home. Similarly, the doubtful aspects of Moll's repentance militate against the idea that she experienced any spiritual transformation. After all, she began to show signs of remorse for her criminal behavior, not when she was first brought to prison or even when she was sentenced to death, but only when she realized that appearing to be a penitent might help her to extricate herself from her situation.

Part Twelve: A Happy Reunion

Summary

After Moll's sentence was reduced from death to transportation, she learned that Jemy and his fellow highway robbers had been able to bribe some of the witnesses against them. However, all three were still being held in Newgate while the authorities continued to investigate their case. Moll pretended that she planned to testify against Jemy and, by means of this subterfuge, managed to see him alone in a cell.

Jemy was at first ashamed to see Moll because he had no idea that she had taken up a life of crime. However, when she informed him of some of the particulars of her history since she had seen him last, he was perfectly willing to describe his adventures as a highway man. After Jemy had provided Moll with a detailed account of the offenses he had committed, she gave him a somewhat incomplete and misleading chronicle of the events which had led to her arrest. Having exchanged stories, both began to consider what they might do in order to live together again. Moll argued that Jemy should do his best to get himself transported with her to the colonies. Although Jemy initially maintained that hanging would be a much more noble fate than transportation, he gradually came around to Moll's point of view.

Weeks later, Moll was placed on a convict ship bound for Virginia. Before the boat sailed, the governess came to Moll's aid once again. The governess first made sure that Moll had plenty of money and all the supplies she might need to begin a new life in Virginia. Then, through tremendous efforts, she managed to arrange for Jemy to be placed on the very same ship as Moll. By the time Jemy arrived on board, Moll, who had at first been confined below deck with the other convicts, was allowed to roam freely about the ship.

Analysis

What is most significant about Moll's reunion with Jemy is that, despite her genuine devotion to him, she still did not provide him with a truthful account of her history. Moreover, she failed to tell him the details of her criminal past even though he had been engaged in exactly the same activities. One way to make sense of

Moll's lack of candor is to compare it to her episode of horse stealing. Just as she stole the horse out of sheer habit, she seems to lie as a matter of course.

On a deeper level, Moll's reticence indicates that she is simply incapable of trusting anyone, including the only man she had ever loved in her life. Moll certainly had some reason to mistrust Jemy. He was, after all, a highway robber, and his somewhat silly preoccupation with his reputation as a gentleman indicates the weakness of his character, as does the way he allowed Moll to determine his future. Moll, with her typical penetration, realized that he was a man who was well-meaning, but who required manipulation. Thus she told him only as much as she had to in order to gain the upper hand in their relationship. Moreover, she seems to have realized that a weak man who would submit to her direction would be an ideal companion for a woman saddled with such a criminal past.

Part Thirteen: Off to America

Summary

As soon as they were together on board, Moll and Jemy made a survey of their money and possessions. Jemy explained that he had been forced to spend a great deal of the money he had amassed through thieving in order to live like a gentleman in Newgate and to bribe the witnesses against him. Nevertheless, he had a significant sum left over to add to their stock. Moll, on the other hand, had an enormous amount of money, as well as a large cache of jewelry, linen, and silver, hidden in a chest on the boat. Moreover, the governess had arranged to have all of the tools and implements they would need to set themselves up as planters shipped to the colonies under Moll's real name.

The couple decided to employ some of their money to make their journey more tolerable. Consequently, before the ship set sail, the governess came aboard to convince the captain to provide them with comfortable accommodations. In the course of her conversation with the captain, the governess discovered that he would be willing, not only to make certain that Moll and Jemy would enjoy their voyage, but also to secure their freedom immediately after they reached their destination. Once the captain, who turned out to be extremely polite and solicitous, had received his compensation, he treated Moll and Jemy as if they had come aboard his ship, not as convicts, but as paying passengers with all the rights and liberties of free citizens.

When the ship docked in Virginia forty-two days later, the captain set about relieving Moll and Jemy of their obligation to pay their debt to society by working as indentured servants. First, he had a wealthy planter purchase their services, then he arranged for the planter to grant them their liberty. For this favor, Moll and Jemy gave the captain six thousand pounds of tobacco and a great deal of money. Everyone came away from the transaction entirely satisfied. Possessed of their liberty, as well as a considerable amount of stock and supplies, Jemy and Moll were eager to begin their new life.

Soon after their arrival, Moll discovered that her brother lived on a plantation very close to the warehouse in which she and Jemy stored their supplies. Though Moll was extremely reluctant to re-encounter her brother, she wandered around the area to see if she could gather further information. A local woman who accompanied her on her rambles told her that a young man owned the plantation and lived there along with his aged father. The woman also told her a story that had long circulated about a beautiful woman who had once been the old man's wife, but who had left him to go to England and had never been heard of since. According to the woman, the old man's wife was rumored to have left him because she found out that she was actually his sister.

Moll was profoundly affected by this all too familiar story. Indeed, while the woman was telling her this tale, the young owner of the plantation, the man Moll knew to be her son, passed by with his elderly father. The old man was too blind to recognize Moll, but she knew without a doubt that this was her brother. Unable to reveal herself to her family, Moll waited until they were out of sight and then kissed the ground her son had walked on. She longed to go after him, to make herself known as his mother, and to clasp him in her arms. However, the thought that she would have to tell her son of the unnatural circumstances which led to his birth stilled her maternal instincts.

Although Moll was upset by the sight of her son and her brother, she was not too distracted to ask her companion about the economic standing of her relations or to find out if the woman had any information about the legacy Moll's mother had promised to leave her so many years before. The woman told Moll that the old man's mother had left her daughter a large piece of land and a sizable fortune. She also said that, since the old man had grown increasingly demented after finding out that he had mistakenly married his sister, his son had been entrusted to transfer the legacy to his mother should she ever return. At that point, Moll began to realize how much she would lose if she failed to renew her relationship with her son.

Analysis

This part of the story is particularly out of keeping with Defoe's assertion that his purpose in transcribing Moll's story was to illustrate that those who stray from the path of virtue always meet with an awful fate. Both Moll and Jemy used their ill-gotten gains, first to buy their freedom, and then to set themselves up as wealthy planters. Both managed, in other words, to profit handsomely from their many misdeeds. Moreover, they flourished even though neither had shown any real remorse or tried to make amends for any of the harm each had caused.

Moll's unrestrained materialism also figures prominently in this chapter. Her reunion with Jemy is, for example, described almost exclusively in economic terms. Even more significantly, she recognized how profoundly she desired to renew her ties with her son, not when she saw him walking with his father, but when she learned that her mother had left her a great deal of property and realized that she could not get hold of her inheritance any other way.

Part Fourteen: Rich at Last

Summary

After Moll found out about her inheritance, she wondered if she might be able to reunite with her relatives without letting Jemy

Part Fourteen

know about her unnatural relationship with her brother. Having given the matter a great deal of thought, she decided to convince her husband that they ought to move someplace where no one could possibly discover their criminal backgrounds. Moll's scheme was to come back to Virginia after they had established themselves in their new home. That way, she would be able to visit her son and brother, and Jemy would be too far away to discover the true purpose of her journey.

Jemy was at first reluctant to move. However, when Moll pointed out how much less anxious they would feel among strangers, Jemy agreed that leaving Virginia made a great deal of sense. Consequently, after much debate, they decided to buy a plantation in the colony of Maryland, a place that Moll favored because the warmer climate was suited to a woman of her advanced age. Though Moll initially considered sending Jemy ahead while she made arrangements to meet with her brother and her son, she decided that he was simply too indolent and impractical to make his way alone in new surroundings. Therefore, she determined that she would accompany him to Maryland and then return at the earliest opportunity.

In less than a year, Moll managed to set up an admirable household on a prosperous plantation, to hire over fifty field hands and servants, and to plant many acres of tobacco, which, at the time, could be expected to bring in considerable profits. Reviewing their great good fortune in their new home, she and Jemy reflected on how much better off they were, not only in comparison to what they had faced in Newgate, but in comparison to even the most prosperous portions of their criminal careers.

The security of their situation in Maryland convinced Moll that she should sail back across the Chesapeake Bay to Virginia in order to see her brother and her son. Before she arrived, Moll sent a message to her brother, telling him how anxious she was to meet with him and how tenderly she anticipated her reunion with her long lost son. Because Moll's brother was too blind to read anymore, the message was delivered directly to her son, who, having learned that his mother was still alive, rushed to see her straight away. After a joyful reunion, Moll's son told her that his father was too infirm and feeble-minded to withstand the news of her return.

Consequently, both he and his mother agreed that it would be better not to subject the old man to such a traumatic revelation.

Over the next five weeks, Moll enjoyed a delightful visit with her son. In fact, she was so taken by his intelligence and thoughtfulness, she almost began to wish that she did not have to go back to Jemy in Maryland. However, even though her son begged her to remain with him, she realized that she loved her Lancashire husband, as she liked to call Jemy, too much to leave him alone to fend for himself. Thus, after her son made sure his mother had collected her inheritance, he loaded her down with gifts to carry back to her plantation and arranged for his own ship to transport her back across the bay.

In the years that followed, Moll and Jemy prospered beyond their wildest dreams. While Jemy took up hunting and other activities appropriate for a landed gentleman, Moll expertly managed their plantation and kept their household running smoothly. The rich land, as well as the fact that they had settled among people who were also engaged in starting new lives, made them feel happier and more secure than they had ever been before.

Given the immediate success they had achieved as planters, Moll wrote to her governess and requested her to use the money she had left back in England to buy fine clothes, guns, wigs, and other finished goods unavailable in the colonies. Furnished with these niceties and blessed with abundant harvests, Moll and Jemy grew more contented every year. Meanwhile, having heard that her brother had died, Moll felt free to tell Jemy of the unnatural relationship that had led to the birth of her ever-dutiful son. Jemy received this information with great understanding and declared that none of it lay Moll open to any degree of blame.

At the close of her narrative, Moll describes how she and Jemy decided to return to England to live out their old age. Although Moll was over seventy and her husband was sixty-eight, both enjoyed good health and vigorous spirits. Moreover, in view of how long they had been away from England, both believed that they no longer faced any danger of arrest or prosecution for their previous crimes. Thus, having spent eight years in America, they returned to their native country and, in light of their liberty, happiness, and wealth, resolved to spend their final years in genuine repentance for the wicked lives they had lived.

Part Fourteen 75

Analysis

In view of the massive fortune Moll accumulated during the most honest period in her life, Defoe's conclusion seems to be that it is possible for human beings to rescue themselves from moral corruption, but only if they enjoy access to enormous wealth. By the time Moll actually abandoned her habitual tendency to practice deception, she had gained far more than mere security. Possessed of an extensive estate, surrounded by dozens of servants, and furnished with luxuries available only to the aristocracy, Moll had risen high above her childhood ambition to become an independent 'gentlewoman.' Her husband Jemy had likewise reached a social position far removed from his previous occupation. Having once wasted his meager savings trying to pose as a gentleman, he ended up with all of the trappings of nobility, including fancy wigs, ornate swords, and other ostentatious possessions. Moll mentions at various points in this part of her autobiography that she was glad to have left behind her life of crime, but, in keeping with the economic motivations which are stressed throughout the novel, she dwells most on the riches she gained near the end of her life.

Note also that Moll's reformation never inspired her to achieve any positive good. Instead, her highest accomplishment, from a moral point of view, was simply to refrain from wicked deeds. Neither she nor Jemy ever provided anyone else with any sort of assistance; rather, after they grew rich, they merely stopped being bad. Thus, the happy ending Defoe devised for *Moll Flanders* suggests that the relentless pursuit of wealth may not enable individuals to realize any truly admirable goals, but, when their pursuits are successful, it minimizes their inclination to violate the rules of morality and ignore the laws of property. To some extent, the relative degree of honesty Moll achieved at the end of her life supports her contention that she would have been a much better person had she not been born into poverty in Newgate Prison. By breaking off the story at this point, however, Defoe leaves it to the reader to decide whether it is right or wrong for individuals to define economic prosperity as a precondition for personal integrity.

Study Questions

1. What was Moll's view of Newgate Prison after she had been there for a while?
2. What finally inspired Moll to repent of her life of crime?
3. When Moll's sentence of death was lifted, what alternative sentence did she receive?
4. What did Moll manage to take with her on her second voyage to Virginia?
5. What happened to Moll and Jemy when they first arrived in America?
6. Which of her relatives did Moll encounter upon her return to Virginia?

Part Fourteen

7. Where did Moll and Jemy buy land after they arrived in Virginia?
8. What did Moll receive from the governess after she and Jemy moved to their new home?
9. How long was Moll's second stay in America?
10. Where do Moll and Jemy live out their old age?

Answers

1. At first, Moll was horrified by the dismal conditions in Newgate Prison, but, after a time, she began to find Newgate not only tolerable but almost agreeable.
2. Moll became a penitent after she heard a minister describe the benefits she would derive from repentance. Defoe leaves it up to the reader to decide whether or not she had truly been saved.
3. Like her mother had been, Moll was sentenced to several years of indentured servitude in America.
4. Moll somehow managed to take a trunk full of gold, silver, jewelry, and fine linen with her on the prison ship.
5. The captain of the prison ship arranged for a wealthy planter to buy Moll and Jemy's contracts for indentured servitude (forced labor). Immediately after the couple met the planter, he proceeded to set them free.
6. Soon after she arrived in Virginia, Moll caught sight of her brother, who had once been her husband, and one of her sons, whom she had not seen since his early childhood. Moll did not make herself known to her relatives, but she became determined to introduce herself to her son when she learned that he could help her procure a legacy left to her by her mother.
7. Because Moll did not want to live in close proximity to her relations in Virginia, she and Jemy purchased a tobacco plantation in the colony of Maryland.

Part Fourteen 79

8. The governess sent Moll a cargo of finished goods, including guns, swords, wigs, linen, gowns, cloaks, and other trappings of aristocratic life. Thus Moll and Jemy managed to set themselves up as members of the highest social class.
9. Moll spent eight years in America after she arrived for the second time, the same amount of time she had spent there earlier in her life.
10. Because they were sure that they could no longer be prosecuted for any of their previous crimes, Moll and Jemy returned to England to live out the rest of their lives.

Suggested Essay Topics

1. Explore the validity of Moll's repentance. Be sure to note exactly when and how Moll decided to show remorse for her sins.
2. Discuss the implications of the prosperity Moll achieved at the end of her life. Explain what you think Defoe meant to suggest by emphasizing how well-to-do Moll became in her old age.
3. Discuss Defoe's view of the American colonies by comparing Moll's first sojourn in America with her second stay there.

SECTION SEVEN

Sample Analytical Paper Topics

Topic #1

Discuss the critique of economic self-interest contained in *Moll Flanders*.

Outline

I. Thesis Statement: *In* Moll Flanders, *Daniel Defoe explores the social and psychological consequences of individual greed.*

II. The role of economic motivation in *Moll Flanders*
   A. Historical Setting
   B. Social circumstances of the main character
   C. Psychological motivation of the main character

III. Moll's pursuit of wealth
   A. Her first affair
   B. Her adventures in marriage
   C. Her life of crime

IV. Moll's materialistic approach to moral salvation
   A. Her repentance
   B. Her move to America
   C. Her prosperous old age

V. Conclusion: Defoe seems to suggest that material ambition can lead both to moral corruption and to spectacular financial success

Sample Analytical Paper Topics

Topic #2

Explore Defoe's approach to criminal activity in *Moll Flanders*.

Outline

I. Thesis Statement: *In* Moll Flanders, *Daniel Defoe provides profound insight into eighteenth-century British views of criminal behavior.*

II. Historical Background
   A. Defoe's familiarity with Newgate Prison
   B. Defoe's preoccupation with ingenious criminals

III. Moll's descent into crime
   A. Moll's criminal activities
   B. Moll's view of her own behavior
   C. The psychological effects of Moll's criminal acts

IV. The legal and penal system as depicted in *Moll Flanders*
   A. Moll's encounters with the law
   B. Moll's incarceration in Newgate Prison
   C. Moll's first and second sentencing

V. Defoe's conception of the American colonies as a refuge for criminals
   A. Moll's mother's life after her transportation to America
   B. Moll and Jemy's life after their transportation to America

VI. Conclusion: In some ways, Defoe seems to romanticize criminal life.

Topic #3

Examine the critique of aristocracy contained in *Moll Flanders*.

Outline

I. Thesis Statement: *Throughout* Moll Flanders, *Defoe criticizes the aristocratic notion that property and social standing should be inherited rather than earned.*

II. Historical Background
   A. The role of aristocracy in eighteenth-century British society
   B. The rise of the stock market, the commercialization of agriculture, and the growth of international trade
   C. The conflicts between traditional and modern ideas about individual prosperity
III. Moll's encounters with aristocracy early in her life
   A. Moll's childhood ambition to become a 'gentlewoman'
   B. The contrast between Moll and the daughters in her wealthy foster family
IV. Moll's efforts to adopt an aristocratic disguise
   A. Moll's ability to pose as a wealthy widow
   B. Moll's attraction to the trappings of aristocratic life
V. The depiction of male aristocrats in *Moll Flanders*
   A. The dishonesty of the elder son in Moll's foster family
   B. Jemy's aristocratic pretensions
   C. The conduct of the gentleman of Bath
   D. The behavior of the baronet
VI. Moll and Jemy's rise to aristocratic standing at the end of *Moll Flanders*
   A. Moll's contribution to their estate
   B. Jemy's pursuits as a wealthy planter
   C. The fortune Moll and Jemy carry back to England
VII. Conclusion: In *Moll Flanders*, Defoe interprets aristocratic identity as a superficial disguise.

Topic #4
Examine Defoe's view of women as evidenced in *Moll Flanders*.

Sample Analytical Paper Topics

Outline

I. Thesis Statement: *The title character of* Moll Flanders *has frequently been described as an embodiment of capitalist consciousness. This paper will explore why Defoe chose a female character to play that role.*

II. Historical Background
   A. The allegedly effeminate aspects of aristocratic society
   B. The eighteenth century conception of getting and spending as essentially feminine activities
   C. The eighteenth century British fascination with female criminals

III. The entrepreneurial aspects of Moll's character
   A. Moll's materialistic approach to relationships
   B. Moll's willingness to give herself to wealthy men
   C. Moll's practical approach to crime

IV. Moll as a symbol of commercial success
   A. Her intelligence
   B. Her lack of pretension
   C. Her audacity

V. Moll as a symbol of selfish ambition
   A. Her vanity
   B. Her appetites
   C. Her willingness to practice deception

VI. Moll as an embodiment of commercial consciousness
   A. Moll as a creature of limitless desire
   B. Moll as a victim of impersonal social forces

VII. Conclusion: *In Moll Flanders,* Defoe confirms the stereotypical view of women as sources of moral corruption and victims of circumstance.

SECTION EIGHT

Bibliography

Cockburn, J.S. *Crime in England, 1500-1800*. Cambridge: Cambridge University Press, 1977.

Defoe, Daniel. *Daniel Defoe*. J.T. Boulton, editor. New York: Schocken Books, 1965.

Defoe, Daniel. *Moll Flanders*. Harmondsworth: Penguin Books, 1978.

Hay, Douglas, editor. *Albion's Fatal Tree: Crime and Society in Eighteenth-Century England*. London: A. Lane Publishers, 1975.
Kelly, Edward H., editor. *Moll Flanders: An Authoritative Text, Backgrounds and Sources, Criticism*. W.W. Norton & Company, 1973.

Meir, Thomas Keith. *Defoe and the Defense of Commerce*. Victoria, B.C.: English Literary Studies, The University of Victoria, 1987.

Plumb, J.H. *England in the Eighteenth Century*. Harmondsworth: Penguin Books, 1978.

Schonhorn, Manuel. *Defoe's Politics: Parliament, Power, Kingship, and Robinson Crusoe*. Cambridge, Cambridge University Press, 1991.

MAXnotes®

REA's Literature Study Guides

MAXnotes® are student-friendly. They offer a fresh look at masterpieces of literature, presented in a lively and interesting fashion. **MAXnotes®** offer the essentials of what you should know about the work, including outlines, explanations and discussions of the plot, character lists, analyses, and historical context. **MAXnotes®** are designed to help you think independently about literary works by raising various issues and thought-provoking ideas and questions. Written by literary experts who currently teach the subject, **MAXnotes®** enhance your understanding and enjoyment of the work.

Available **MAXnotes®** include the following:

Absalom, Absalom!
The Aeneid of Virgil
Animal Farm
Antony and Cleopatra
As I Lay Dying
As You Like It
The Autobiography of Malcolm X
The Awakening
Beloved
Beowulf
Billy Budd
The Bluest Eye, A Novel
Brave New World
The Canterbury Tales
The Catcher in the Rye
The Color Purple
The Crucible
Death in Venice
Death of a Salesman
The Divine Comedy I: Inferno
Dubliners
Emma
Euripedes' Electra & Medea
Frankenstein
Gone with the Wind
The Grapes of Wrath
Great Expectations
The Great Gatsby
Gulliver's Travels
Hamlet
Hard Times

Heart of Darkness
Henry IV, Part I
Henry V
The House on Mango Street
Huckleberry Finn
I Know Why the Caged Bird Sings
The Iliad
Invisible Man
Jane Eyre
Jazz
The Joy Luck Club
Jude the Obscure
Julius Caesar
King Lear
Les Misérables
Lord of the Flies
Macbeth
The Merchant of Venice
The Metamorphoses of Ovid
The Metamorphosis
Middlemarch
A Midsummer Night's Dream
Moby-Dick
Moll Flanders
Mrs. Dalloway
Much Ado About Nothing
My Antonia
Native Son
1984
The Odyssey
Oedipus Trilogy

Of Mice and Men
On the Road
Othello
Paradise Lost
A Passage to India
Plato's Republic
Portrait of a Lady
A Portrait of the Artist as a Young Man
Pride and Prejudice
A Raisin in the Sun
Richard II
Romeo and Juliet
The Scarlet Letter
Sir Gawain and the Green Knight
Slaughterhouse-Five
Song of Solomon
The Sound and the Fury
The Stranger
The Sun Also Rises
A Tale of Two Cities
Taming of the Shrew
The Tempest
Tess of the D'Urbervilles
Their Eyes Were Watching God
To Kill a Mockingbird
To the Lighthouse
Twelfth Night
Uncle Tom's Cabin
Waiting for Godot
Wuthering Heights

RESEARCH & EDUCATION ASSOCIATION
61 Ethel Road W. • Piscataway, New Jersey 08854
Phone: (908) 819-8880

Please send me more information about MAXnotes®.

Name _____

Address _____

City _____ State _____ Zip _____

THE BEST TEST PREPARATION FOR THE

SAT II: Subject Test

WRITING

by the Staff of Research & Education Association

6 Full-Length Exams

- Every question based on the current exams
- The ONLY test preparation book with detailed explanations to every question
- Far more comprehensive than any other test preparation book

Includes a Comprehensive COURSE REVIEW of Writing, emphasizing all major topics found on the exam

REA *Research & Education Association*

Available at your local bookstore or order directly from us by sending in coupon below.

RESEARCH & EDUCATION ASSOCIATION
61 Ethel Road W., Piscataway, New Jersey 08854
Phone: (908) 819-8880

VISA **MasterCard**

Charge Card Number

☐ Payment enclosed
☐ Visa ☐ Master Card

Expiration Date: _____ / _____
                    Mo   Yr

Please ship REA's **"SAT II: Writing"** @ $13.95 plus $4.00 for shipping.

Name _____

Address _____

City _____ State _____ Zip _____

REA's Test Preps
The Best in Test Preparation

REA "Test Preps" are far **more** comprehensive than any other test preparation series
Each book contains up to **eight** full-length practice exams based on the most recent exams
Every type of question likely to be given on the exams is included
Answers are accompanied by **full** and **detailed** explanations

REA has published over 60 Test Preparation volumes in several series. They include:

Advanced Placement Exams (APs)
Biology
Calculus AB & Calculus BC
Chemistry
Computer Science
English Language & Composition
English Literature & Composition
European History
Government & Politics
Physics
Psychology
Spanish Language
United States History

College Level Examination Program (CLEP)
American History I
Analysis & Interpretation of Literature
College Algebra
Freshman College Composition
General Examinations
Human Growth and Development
Introductory Sociology
Principles of Marketing

SAT II: Subject Tests
American History
Biology
Chemistry
French
German
Literature

SAT II: Subject Tests (continued)
Mathematics Level IC, IIC
Physics
Spanish
Writing

Graduate Record Exams (GREs)
Biology
Chemistry
Computer Science
Economics
Engineering
General
History
Literature in English
Mathematics
Physics
Political Science
Psychology
Sociology

ACT - American College Testing Assessment

ASVAB - Armed Service Vocational Aptitude Battery

CBEST - California Basic Educational Skills Test

CDL - Commercial Driver's License Exam

CLAST - College Level Academic Skills Test

ELM - Entry Level Mathematics

ExCET - Exam for Certification of Educators in Texas

FE (EIT) - Fundamentals of Engineering Exam

FE Review - Fundamentals of Engineering Review

GED - High School Equivalency Diploma Exam (US & Canadian editions)

GMAT - Graduate Management Admission Test

LSAT - Law School Admission Test

MAT - Miller Analogies Test

MCAT - Medical College Admission Test

MSAT - Multiple Subjects Assessment for Teachers

NTE - National Teachers Exam

PPST - Pre-Professional Skills Tests

PSAT - Preliminary Scholastic Assessment Test

SAT I - Reasoning Test

SAT I - Quick Study & Review

TASP - Texas Academic Skills Program

TOEFL - Test of English as a Foreign Language

RESEARCH & EDUCATION ASSOCIATION
61 Ethel Road W. • Piscataway, New Jersey 08854
Phone: (908) 819-8880

Please send me more information about your Test Prep Books

Name _____

Address _____

City _____ State _____ Zip _____

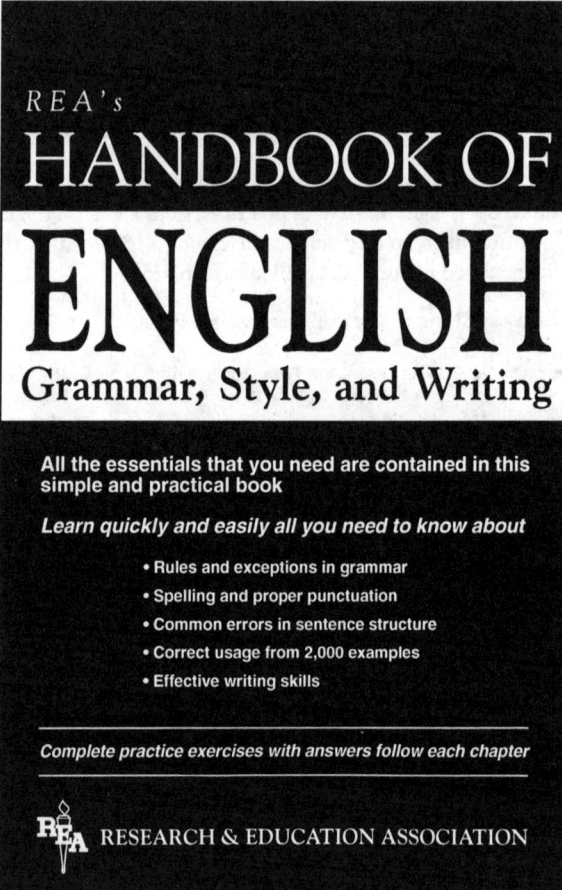

Available at your local bookstore or order directly from us by sending in coupon below.

RESEARCH & EDUCATION ASSOCIATION
61 Ethel Road W., Piscataway, New Jersey 08854
Phone: (908) 819-8880

☐ Payment enclosed
☐ Visa ☐ Master Card

Charge Card Number

Expiration Date: ____ / ____
                   Mo   Yr

Please ship **"Handbook of English"** @ $17.95 plus $4.00 for shipping.

Name _____

Address _____

City _____ State _____ Zip _____

Available at your local bookstore or order directly from us by sending in coupon below.

RESEARCH & EDUCATION ASSOCIATION
61 Ethel Road W., Piscataway, New Jersey 08854
Phone: (908) 819-8880

☐ Payment enclosed
☐ Visa ☐ Master Card

Charge Card Number

Expiration Date: ____ / ____
                  Mo   Yr

Please ship REA's **"AP English Literature & Composition"** @ $15.95 plus $4.00 for shipping.

Name _____

Address _____

City _____ State _____ Zip _____

QUICK STUDY & REVIEW FOR THE NEW SAT I

for students with limited study time and those who want a "refresher" before taking the test

REA *Research & Education Association*

Available at your local bookstore or order directly from us by sending in coupon below.

RESEARCH & EDUCATION ASSOCIATION
61 Ethel Road W., Piscataway, New Jersey 08854
Phone: (908) 819-8880

VISA **MasterCard**

Charge Card Number

☐ Payment enclosed
☐ Visa ☐ Master Card

Expiration Date: _____ / _____
                      Mo   Yr

Please ship REA's **"Quick Study & Review for the SAT I"** @ $8.95 plus $2.00 for shipping.

Name _____

Address _____

City _____ State _____ Zip _____